Gentle and Passionate

Gentle and Passionate

Reflections from a Year as Moderator

Andrew R C McLellan

For Jean - Bob

in friendship

Andrew

May 2001

Saint Andrew Press

To John and Isabel
chaplains extraordinary

First published in 2001 by
SAINT ANDREW PRESS
121 George Street
Edinburgh EH2 4YN

ISBN 0 7152 0797 0

British Library Cataloguing in Publication Data
A catalogue record for this book is available from the British Library.

Typeset in Scotland
by McColl Productions, Edinburgh

Printed and bound in the United Kingdom
by Bell & Bain Ltd., Glasgow

The quotation on p. 113, from Hugh MacDiarmid, *Collected Poems of Hugh MacDiarmid* (1967), is gratefully reproduced with the permission of Carcanet Press Limited.

CONTENTS

FOREWORD
by the Director of Christian Aid

HERE is a new book by someone who saw his leadership as a challenge for himself and the church in relating faith to the concerns of the world. His sermons show the breadth of his interests and the passion and conviction that he brings to his ministry.

During his term as Moderator, Andrew discharged his traditional and important duties with humility and integrity. He also travelled overseas to see the work of the churches, visit their development projects and new initiatives, and meet local leaders. This was an integral part of his role – to show solidarity with people in need and a willingness to listen.

Why should the Moderator go to Africa? As part of his witness, Andrew was keen to visit the Caribbean, Malawi and Palestine/Israel to show that the church cares for all people. Here is a man of passion – willing to get involved.

These sermons are a challenge for us today. What does it mean to be Christian in a world of poverty, war, injustice and marginalisation? Andrew's collection should help us reflect – how can we put our faith into action?

Together we can build a better world. This book contains signs of hope and commitment by many. We need to be agents for global transformation. In doing so, we are contributing to building a more just, inclusive and sustainable world in the perspective of the reign of God.

Daleep Mukarji
April 2001

INTRODUCTION

EVERY year, the Church of Scotland chooses someone to be Moderator of the General Assembly. For twelve months, the Moderator speaks and broadcasts and writes and preaches; for twelve months, the Moderator is entertained and entertains and meets and welcomes and listens; for twelve months, the Moderator is treated with the greatest respect and has a great deal of fun. The year is filled with opportunities and kindnesses. The secret is for the Moderator to take the office very seriously without taking himself or herself too seriously: one of the most distinguished of them all, George MacLeod, remarked: 'Being Moderator is great so long as you don't inhale!'

This book contains some of the things I said during my year as Moderator of the General Assembly from May 2000. From the beginning, I wanted to make sure that preaching was at the forefront of the year's work; so the bulk of this book is sermons. The first section includes the sermon preached at the Assembly Service in St Giles' Cathedral in Edinburgh; the brief preaching at the opening of each section of the Assembly, based on those parables of St Luke's Gospel which do not occur anywhere else; and the Closing Address. The second section is made up of sermons preached throughout the year: some were for special occasions or anniversaries or particular places, and others for the normal worship of congregations of the Church of Scotland across the country. Finally, I have included some addresses given in a variety of circumstances. One of the projects I undertook as Moderator was to visit every prison in Scotland: some reflections on this are in the last section of the book.

At the General Assembly, I said: 'Let us pray for a passionate church in a gentle Scotland'. Throughout the year that followed, I tried to keep that hope before me. The contents of this book are less gentle than I would like, and less passionate than they should be; but I have never been in doubt in this year that these remain the qualities which the Church needs and which, in particular, its preachers need. There are several references in the book to Jean Vanier, the founder of L'Arche. It was one of the supreme privileges, not just of this year, but of my life, to introduce him to the General Assembly. I hope that it will be possible to hear something of his gentleness and his passion in the pages that follow.

Andrew R C McLellan
Edinburgh
March 2001

The General Assembly

Sermon in St Giles' Cathedral
Parables of St Luke
Closing Address

SERMON IN ST GILES' CATHEDRAL

Divine contentment and divine discontent

THIS sermon was preached at the opening service of the General Assembly.

Luke 12:16–21. The parable of the rich fool.

For two reasons, it is difficult to imagine yourself as a rich fool! You will have to do that this morning, but begin with something more straightforward. Imagine yourself as an ancient Chinese stone-cutter.

One day, an ancient Chinese stone-cutter passed the house of a wealthy merchant. 'How powerful that man must be!' he thought enviously. 'I wish I could be that merchant.' To his surprise, he suddenly became the merchant, enjoying more luxury and power than he had ever dreamed of. But soon a high official passed by, carried in a sedan chair and escorted by soldiers and a bowing procession. 'How powerful that official is!' he thought. 'I wish I could be that high official.' Then he became that official, carried everywhere in his sedan chair. One hot summer's day, he felt very uncomfortable in his sticky chair and looked up at the sun shining proudly. 'How powerful that sun is! I wish I could be the sun!'

Then he became the sun, shining fiercely on everyone. But a huge black cloud moved between him and the earth, and he could no longer shine below. 'How powerful that cloud is! I wish I could be that cloud.' Then he became the cloud, flooding the fields and villages. But soon he found he was being pushed away by some great force – the wind. 'I wish I could be the wind.' Then he blew tiles off houses and uprooted trees. But soon he ran up against something that would not move before him: a huge, towering stone. 'How powerful that stone is!' Then he became the stone, more powerful than anything else on earth.

But as he stood there, he heard the sound of a hammer pounding a chisel into the solid rock, and he felt himself changed. 'What could be more powerful than I, the stone?' he thought. He looked down and saw far below him the figure of a stone-cutter.[1]

An ancient Chinese stone-cutter: discontented where he might have been content. This is what envy does to you, what greed does to you. Whether you are an ancient Chinese stone-cutter or a modern Scottish Moderator, whether you are a rich fool or a poor fool, the amount of energy which you put into lusting after what you do not have and will not have and cannot have – the amount of absolutely pointless and useless energy which you put into being greedy and envious – is in direct disproportion to any good that such effort and energy does to you or to anyone else or to the world.

Can a church be discontented where it might have been content? A church can certainly be envious. The Church of Scotland might be warned against simple envy of the attention which some sections of the press like to pay to two outspoken Scottish bishops. Or envy of past days of glory. Or envy of the dynamism of elders in American Presbyterianism or the growth of Christianity in Africa. All of this is just plain envy and discontent.

But it is the place where you are standing now that is holy ground, the place where you are to meet God. The place to which God has called you. The people with whom God has called you. It is where you are and as you are that God means to work some mighty work in you. Oh Church of Scotland, learn from an ancient Jewish tent-maker: 'I have learned to be content with whatever I have. I can do all things through him who strengthens me' (Phil. 4:11–13).

Now you are ready to imagine yourself as a rich fool. You are the story of Jesus we heard this morning. I have vast possessions. What will I do? The problem, though I don't realise it, is not the size of my harvest but my insistence on gathering it all and storing it for my own use. Indeed, throughout my story it is all the first person: *my* crops, *my* barns, *my* grain, *my* goods and *my* soul. Anyway, I know the solution. Bigger and better barns: more and more room for all my stuff. Then it will be relax, eat, drink and be merry. There is no-one else in my story. Just me and my things. Until God speaks: 'You fool! This very night, your life is being demanded of you. And the things you have prepared, whose will they be?'

They are both greedy men, the stone-cutter and the fool; but their difference is more interesting than their similarity. For the downfall of the rich man in Jesus' story is that he was content where he should have been discontented. Just the opposite of the first man: the second story is about one who was content where he should have been discontented. He is so insufferably smug.

Complacency when others around you suffer has an ugliness all of its own. The thought of sharing some of his rich harvest with persons in need never entered the head of the rich fool. Every 3.6 seconds, someone dies of hunger; out of every four such people, three are under five years old. The only thing worse than the blindness of the man in the story to the needs of others is his contentment with the dreadful crassness of his own life, his own horizons, his own values. In John le Carré's latest best-seller, *Single and Single*, there is an illuminating phrase. Oliver and Heather furnished their house 'when they were buying everything because buying was the only language left to them'.[2] The rich fool has immortal longings in him; he was made to glorify God and enjoy him forever, and he is content with the aspirations of a jellyfish. Pray that you may be delivered from smugness.

Content where he should be discontented. Can a church be like that? A church can certainly be complacent. Forty years ago, the churches in Canada did a brave thing. They invited an unbelieving journalist called Pierre Berton to take a long look at them from the outside and then write a book. His book was a terrible condemnation of complacency; and, while I remember little else of it, the title is with me yet: *The Comfortable Pew*. Oh Church of Scotland, have you the courage to do the same: to invite some shrewd analyst to put your dreams, your aspirations, your very life to exacting examination? However valuable it is to examine ourselves – and this Assembly will be doing plenty of that – we might learn a great deal more from listening to the honest assessment of those who look at us with fresh eyes. I would be so pleased if such a project could somehow be born in my year of office. For a church with comfortable pews is no church at all. It is only a church if it learns never to be content where it should be discontented.

Two stories about contentment and discontent. Two stories pointing to a version of the serenity prayer – the 'contentment prayer'. 'Lord, grant me the serenity to be content when I should be content, and discontented when I should be discontented, and the wisdom to know the difference.'

That's the hard part. When is it Christian to be content, and when is it Christian to be discontented? Which is this morning's way of putting the question above all questions: 'How are we to know the will of God?' Please come to the General Assembly tonight, when you might just learn the answer, or at least learn where the answer is to be found. For it will be with great pride that I will welcome tonight one of the spiritual giants of Christianity today, Jean Vanier. And he will tell us that

God will speak to us in the poor and the weak and the vulnerable and the helpless; and if we listen to them we will know the will of God. And then we will know the right time to be discontented and the right time to be content.

Jean Vanier founded L'Arche – communities of handicapped people and those who share their lives. He wrote:

> We are all loved by God, but the gospel shows us that the poor, the weak and the marginalised have a special place in God's heart. Just as God called Moses to free the people from slavery, so God calls and sends the assistants of L'Arche to welcome those who are oppressed and suffering rejection because of their mental handicaps. God opens the hearts of assistants to their cry and to the anguish of these weak people. And the mystery is that these people, with all their fragility and weakness, transform the assistants, evangelise them, and call them into the heart of the gospel.[3]

It is the weak, the poor, the marginalised, who transform those who come to listen to them. It is the weak, the poor, the marginalised, who lead the strong into the heart of the gospel. Church of Scotland, let Jean Vanier teach you tonight that it is by listening to the most vulnerable among us that we will hear the voice of God and know the will of God. And true contentment and true discontentment will then be ours.

Yesterday, in the opening act of worship, the Assembly sang 'I, the Lord of sea and sky'. There is a terrific misprint in the *Common Ground* text of that hymn; and I am sad to learn that they propose to correct it in the next edition. The original third verse says: 'I, the lord of wind and flame, I will tend the poor and lame'. This is fine, and you could sing it without noticing it. But the inspired mistake of *Common Ground* gives the splendid 'I, the Lord of wind and flame, I will *send* the poor and lame'. The gospel says that they are the messengers of God.

Send them to the rich fool, o God, before it is too late. Send them to the Church of Scotland, that we may know your will, and we may be discontented, and we may be content.

Notes

1. See Benjamin Hoff, *The Tao of Pooh* (London: Methuen, 1982), pp. 130–1.
2. John le Carré, *Single and Single* (London: Coronet, 2000), p. 83.
3. Jean Vanier, *The Heart of L'Arche* (London: Geoffrey Chapman, 1995), p. 84.

PARABLES OF ST LUKE

The Good Samaritan (Luke 10:25–37)

A WHILE ago, an old man asked me for a lift into town. He had been at his bus stop for ages, and he was late and cold. As we chatted, he asked me how I had spent the day – it was a holiday Monday. I told him that I had driven all the way to visit a friend of mine in hospital in Inverness. 'Very good', said he. 'That's what I like to hear! I had a friend in England who was a bishop; but he never went near his neighbour when he was in hospital. That's professional Christians for you, whereas ordinary chaps like you, who probably never go near a church, are better Christians than the clergy types!'

There is a terrifying point to the story. What the world expects of Christians is that they love. And not just bishops, not just ministers – though the coldness of clerics is a terrible thing – but all of us. Of course, it is wretchedly unfair that this is how the world chooses to judge Christians – except that that is exactly what Jesus said.

There are nine parables in St Luke's gospel which do not occur elsewhere. These nine parables will be our companions through the worship of this Assembly. I hope that they will judge us and renew us. They are among the treasures of the Bible, and point to some of Luke's chief concerns. For Luke, Jesus is the Saviour sent to seek and to save the lost.

The figure of the Good Samaritan hangs over the General Assembly on our first day; and I hope that we will never get away from that figure. He points us to two fundamental questions. How does what we do here, what we decide here, affect the weakest, the poor, the wounded? As you vote, that question must be before you: how does what we decide here affect the weak, the poor, the wounded?

And the figure of the Good Samaritan also asks us this: who are the real outsiders, and who are the real insiders, in the economy of God? Jesus' story was not a comforting story for the priests and the Levites. Where are we to look in today's world for the healing hand of God?

The barren fig-tree (Luke 13:6–9)

THE General Assembly will not find me sympathetic to discussions about the correct date for marking the millennium. But I cannot but be moved by the fact of being the Moderator of the General Assembly of the year 2000. I rejoice that later this year a silver cross is to be presented to the Moderator made by students in Glasgow to mark the year 2000; and I shall look forward to handing that cross on – reluctantly – to the Moderator of 2001.

Let the parable of the barren fig-tree help you to reflect on the meaning of the year 2000. The evangelical meaning of the date is not, I think, to do with triumphalism over twenty centuries of Christianity, nor despair about the disappearance of Christendom drowned in a sea of post-modernism. The Christian meaning of the date is that this year is the year that matters. The parable invites us to see this year as the gift of God's mercy. What matters is not chronology but providence. Providence and judgement. This is the year in which we are to seek the Lord.

It is a story of mercy and of judgement. The fig-tree is to be spared, but it is only to be spared for one more year – for this year. This is the fateful year – no, this is the year of God. Oh for just a little urgency in our debates this week! Alistair Cooke was in Germany in 1935 when Hitler was at the height of his terrifying power. What Cooke remembered from the stunningly effective oratory was the repeated phrase 'it is five minutes to midnight'.

It is five minutes to midnight. This year is the year of God. What if the tree bears no fruit this year? What would you do if you had only a year left to live, only a short time in which to make up for the wrongs done and opportunities missed? The old monks used to say: 'If you knew you were to die tonight, what would you do? Now, go ahead and do it.'

The lost coin (Luke 15:8–10)

(The General Assembly communion service)

LIBERAL Christians hear that parable one way; conservative Christians hear it another way. What I want this morning is that you should hear this parable in a different way.

So if you feel that your natural theological inclination is conservative, I want you to hear this parable the way liberals understand it. It is a parable about breaking down barriers, about social inclusion. It is quite deliberate that St Luke tells this story after a preface about the company Jesus keeps: 'Now all the tax-collectors and sinners were coming near to listen to him. And the Pharisees and the scribes were grumbling and saying, "This fellow welcomes sinners and eats with them". So he told them this parable.'

The gospel of Jesus Christ is that the kingdom of God belongs to those whom the world rejects. The sign of the new wine of the kingdom of God is that Jesus shares it with sinners and welcomes them. He welcomes them to his table to eat and drink with him. Table fellowship with outcasts is a sign that they are as precious to God as a coin which a woman lost and found again with much rejoicing. This is a parable about the welcome which Jesus Christ offers to the outsider at the communion table.

If you feel that your natural theological inclination is liberal, and that the interpretation which I have just given is what you have always known the parable to mean, then I want you to hear it in another way. It is a parable about redemption, about being found again by God. It is the end of the parable rather than the beginning where the heart of it is to be found. 'Just so, I tell you, there is joy in the presence of the angels of God over one sinner who repents.'

The gospel of Jesus Christ is that all the barriers which your past has built between you and God have been broken down. You are the lost one whom he came to seek and to save. It was for you that Jesus Christ came into the world: for you he struggled and suffered; for you he died; and for you he was raised to life, so that you might be brought back from death to life and feast with him in the kingdom of God. This is a parable about the welcome which Jesus Christ offers to the sinner at the communion table.

So, on either reading, this parable leads you to the communion table. But Jesus never told a story simply to confirm us in our prejudices. He told this parable to ruffle us. Come to the communion table, but come having heard this story of Jesus tell you something new.

The prodigal son (Luke 15:11–32)

YOU know that story so well. But you do not know what you need to know. You do not know if he came to the party or not. He stands leaning up against the door of the house while they roast the veal and pull the party hats out of the crackers. Will he come in?

Sliding Doors is a film which has two plots running side by side. In one, she catches her train and so discovers that her love affair is over; in the other, she misses her train and lives in blissful ignorance. But it turns out that the happy ending does not follow that happy beginning: what looks like disaster can become beautiful.

Jesus invites Israel – pious, frustrated, spoiled, dull Israel – to come to the party. Will he come or not? Is the story one in which he comes to the party and throws his arms around the prodigal, or is it one in which he stays outside and sulks? Is the story one where the principle which is vindicated is that you have to pay for forgiveness, or is it a story in which love covers a multitude of sins? Israel, will you come to the party?

Church of Scotland, will you come to the party? Does the sliding door open to welcome you to a liberation, and an embracing of the failures, and a recognition that your own repentance is more important than your religion, and a celebration of the gracious love of God in great laughter? Or does the sliding door close to contain you in a religion of duty and nostalgia, and keeping other outsiders outside and making sure that they don't get away with anything, and a sad contentment with the way things have always been? Church of Scotland, will you come to the party? Can your piety stand all that redemption?

The unjust steward (Luke 16:1–10)

SOME translations call this the Parable of the Dishonest Manager. I treasure the misprint of an intrusive 'a' in a St Andrew's and St George's Christmas Order of Service a few years ago. Located where we are in the midst of the business sector, the Christmas anthem appeared as 'Come, let us kneel before the manager'!

The picture of management which captured the imagination of the 1990s was a book by Charles Handy called *The Empty Raincoat*. The Assembly Council made good use of the book in their report to this Assembly. Handy's argument is that we were not destined to be empty raincoats, nameless numbers on a payroll, role occupants, the raw material of economics or sociology, statistics in some government report. If that is to be its price, then economic progress is an empty promise. There must be more to life than being an empty raincoat, a non-person, a cog in someone else's great machine. The challenge facing us all is to discover the kind of society in which we can fill that empty raincoat with people, real people. We were made to be human beings.

That seems to me without doubt the work of God; and I am not one who would sneer at management as a career for those who lack the imagination or social conscience to be poets or nurses. Nor do I despise management models of ministry. If management at its best is about filling that empty raincoat with real people, then that is the work of God.

But the parable is still very difficult. When the drawings, which the Assembly has seen, were being prepared for each of these nine parables, I was not surprised that it was the idea for the drawing for this parable which proved most elusive. You can't escape the difficulty that the manager who is commended is a dishonest manager.

Recently, a young man remarked to me after meeting a senior figure in this General Assembly: 'He's pretty street-wise'! That description as a compliment is the traditional interpretation of this parable. The smarter the children of light can be, the better. Faced with impending calamity, the dishonest manager acts decisively to provide for his future. How much more decisively must be the act of those who will stake their all on the coming kingdom of God.

It is not surprising that a variety of explanations are attached to this parable in the Bible. St Luke found it odd as well. I used to despise the explanations of parables which are given by the gospel-writers, for I was confident that they were almost always misunderstandings of the story's meaning. Now, when I am a great deal more dull of brain, and occasionally a little more humble, I am more grateful for what St Luke has to suggest. And until I can find myself entirely satisfied with the explanation of the parable which I have just called traditional, I shall take refuge in what may well be a secondary meaning – but is still a good meaning. St Luke suggests: 'Whoever is faithful in a very little is faithful also in much'. The great American preacher Fred Craddock offers this commentary on that verse:

> Most of us will not this week christen a ship, write a book, end a war, appoint a cabinet, dine with a queen, convert a nation, or be burned at the stake. More likely the week will present no more than a chance to give a cup of water, write a note, visit a nursing home, vote for a county commissioner, teach a Sunday School class, share a meal, tell a child a story, go to choir practice, and feed the neighbour's cat. 'Whoever is faithful in a very little is faithful also in much.'[1]

The rich man and Lazarus (Luke 16:19–31)

IN July I will have the privilege of visiting Malawi, Mozambique and Zambia on behalf of the General Assembly. The visit will be a great celebration of lively faith on the sunlit plains of Africa, and a wretched glimpse of the catastrophe that is poverty. A visit to these countries, as we have heard in this Assembly, is a visit to some of the very poorest people in the world.

Jesus tells a story about a rich man and a poor man. Like several parables – and despite Jülicher and Jeremias and the great critics of an earlier day – it is a story with more than one point. But it is at least a story about denying food to the poor. Put your money where your mouth is. Put your money where his mouth is. The danger of wealth is such a characteristic theme for Luke.

It has been exciting to watch over the last few years as a Biblical idea of jubilee has inspired the churches and the whole world together to demand the cancellation of unrepayable debt as a mark of the millennium and as a new beginning for rich and poor alike. But let us not be dewy-eyed about our idealism. The relations between the world's rich and the world's poor are judged by a story Jesus told about a rich man and a poor man, and by the past and present determination of those of us who are rich to grab all we can and more from the mouths of the poor.

The school in which my wife teaches is a Roman Catholic school, a matter to which the press attaches more importance than I do. A few weeks ago, the pupils of the school did a good thing. They always collect for some project during Lent, and at the end of the term they invited my good friend Archbishop O'Brien and me to the school together. They gave Archbishop O'Brien half of the huge sum they had collected for him to take to a project for the poor in Mexico, and they gave the other half to me to take to a project for the poor in Mozambique. He and I will return to the school to tell them what happened to their money, and I will return to the Assembly next year to tell you. To tell you of seed and sheaves and fish. There is an Irish hymn which begins: 'To Christ the seed, to Christ the sheaves, so into God's barns may we all be brought'.[2]

The unjust judge (Luke 18:1–8)

IN Luke, Jesus extends God's mercy to women as to men, and often departs from the social conventions of his time. Nevertheless, the whole thing is of the first century: recent interpreters like Jane Schaberg have pointed out that Luke still confines women to traditional roles: 'prayerful, quiet, grateful women, supportive of male leadership, forgoing the prophetic ministry'.[3]

Except this woman. For she is not simply the traditional widow, the passive recipient of the charity of others. She is a religious hero. She knows that the well-being of widows, the duty to care for orphans and strangers and the poor, is the very stuff of the religion of her people, and she will not give up. Her prayers rattle the judge's cage: her prayers rattle God's cage. And she will not give up until the kingdom comes and God's will is done.

Beware of seeing her simply as a model of prayerfulness. She is more radical than that. She is the uncomfortable reminder that nothing is more deeply rooted in the religious tradition which begins in the Hebrew Bible than the duty to care for widows. The average age of our population rises inexorably. The average age of our church members rises even faster. The early church was good at caring for those who were old and alone. It is time again for us to listen to this woman.

For there are two characters in the story. There is the praying one, and there is the one who does not listen. Will the Church of Scotland learn to pray? And will the Church of Scotland learn to listen? When King Solomon was offered a gift from God, he asked for 'an understanding heart'. But the more accurate translation is 'a heart skilled to listen'. Now there is something for the Church of Scotland to pray for: for its ministers and deacons, for its elders and its members, for its Courts and its Boards and Committees.

On Sunday morning I quoted the spy novels of John le Carré. Le Carré's great creation is the master spy George Smiley; here is the explanation of George Smiley's peculiar power.

> An intelligence officer is nothing if he has lost the will to listen, and George Smiley, plump, troubled, indefati-

gable George, was the best listener of us all. Smiley could listen with his hooded, sleepy eyes; he could listen by the very inclination of his tubby body, by his stillness and his understanding smile. He could listen because he expected nothing of his fellow souls, criticised nothing, condoned the worst of you long before you had revealed it.[4]

He does not listen, so the unjust judge fails the widow and fails God. Those who learn to listen are learning to love.

The Pharisee and the tax-collector
(Luke 18:9–14)

IF you know and love Garrison Keillor and Lake Wobegon, then you will know and love Father Wilmer, Roman Catholic priest at the delightfully named Our Lady of Perpetual Responsibility. Father Wilmer is very suspicious of Lutherans: they don't really believe anything.

They go to church because they like to drink coffee and they like to eat doughnuts. They sit up in the sanctuary and they don't really have a creed or really believe anything. They get together and they say the pledge of allegiance; they have a talk about sharing; they sing 'Climb every Mountain' and then they go home.[5]

Of course that is America. In Scotland we wouldn't dream of making judgements like that about the things that other people hold sacred, about the faith of other people. We wouldn't dream of passing judgement on other people's religion.

Not if we listened to the parable of the Pharisee and the publican we wouldn't. If we listened to this parable, it would be repentance and charity which we would strive after: repentance and charity and humble faith. We have enough to worry about with our own religion without needing to be superior about what other people believe.

The first of the nine parables which occur only in St Luke is the parable of the Good Samaritan. Last Saturday evening, I said:

> The figure of the Good Samaritan hangs over the General Assembly on our first day; and I hope that we will never get away from that figure. He points us to two fundamental questions. How does what we do here, what we decide here, affect the weakest, the poor, the wounded? As you vote, that question must be before you: how does what we decide here affect the weak, the poor, the wounded?
>
> And the figure of the Good Samaritan also asks us this: who are the real outsiders, and who are the real insiders, in the economy of God? Jesus' story was not a comforting story for the priests and the Levites. Where are we to look in today's world for the healing hand of God?

As now we listen to the last of these nine Lukan parables, the figure of the Good Samaritan still hangs over the General Assembly; and if we have any sense, so does the figure of the tax-collector. Charity and repentance and 'God be merciful to me, a sinner'.

Notes

1. Fred B Craddock, *Luke* (Louisville: Westminster, 1990), p. 192.
2. From *Common Ground*, no. 135.
2. Jane Schaberg, in Carol Newsom and Sharon H Ringe (eds), *The Women's Bible Commentary* (Louisville: Westminster, 1992), p. 275.
4. John le Carré, *The Secret Pilgrim* (London: Coronet, 1994), p. 262.
5. Garrison Keillor, *Fertility: The Six Labors of Father Wilmer* (1990). Transcribed from a tape produced by Highbridge Company, original material © Garrison Keillor 1990, 1991, 1992.

CLOSING ADDRESS AT THE GENERAL ASSEMBLY

A passionate Church in a gentle Scotland

WHEN my father learned that his only son entertained hopes of being a minister, he liked to tell of an old woman. She heard that a boy she had known all his life was becoming a minister, and she remarked: 'I'm not surprised. He was always a harmless kind of lad!'

I pledge myself in the year ahead to do harm. And I hope and pray that the Church of Scotland will do harm. I fervently wish that those whom we have proudly welcomed as new ministers tonight will give the old woman a surprise. For there is a good deal of harm needing to be done. Harm to greed and materialism and selfishness. Harm to godlessness and guilt and fear. Harm to injustice and oppression. Those of us who are harmless in the face of world debt and harmless in the face of grinding poverty in Scotland are not fit to be ministers. I am looking for a passionate Church.

A passionate Church. Is that what we have seen and heard this week? I will remember from this week the plea for passion in the Board of Ministry Report. I will remember the passion of several speakers. But it is not passionate individuals that we need: it is a passionate Church. Moses came from the wilderness full of passion to tell the children of Israel about the exciting and liberating promises of God. 'But they would not listen to Moses because of their broken spirit and cruel slavery' (Exodus 6:9). You must leave this General Assembly passionate: to do harm to that broken spirit and cruel slavery and so

19

let girls and boys, men and women hear the exciting and liberating promises of God.

I pray for a Church that is passionate. Passionate about the weak and about the powerless. On Sunday night, Jean Vanier told us about learning from Antonio, one of those with disability whom he described as 'the most oppressed people in the world'.

> I was a man taught to go up the ladder, to win, be aggressive, do big things. Antonio and others like him have opened my heart: to love is not to give chocolates: to love is to reveal – they have worth, created by God: you are precious. We are called to love people to freedom. Freedom from fear, prejudice, the compulsion to prove I'm better, the need for power and success, freedom to serve.

But also passionate about our own peculiar and particular business. I was shocked recently to discover how few Scottish candidates there are for Scottish theology appointments. There is a Scottish tradition of theology, and if we don't care about nourishing it no-one will. A Scottish tradition that we let die at our peril. This is not just about the training of ministers – although that is important. It is about striving for serious theological engagement with the history and culture and society that is ours. Of course I want to share in all the riches of the world Church and of many theological traditions. But the Church of Scotland needs its own theology, and for that to survive we need to be passionate about theology.

In the Book of Acts, the earliest Christians were so passionate about God that onlookers suspected that they might be drunk. Would anyone in their right minds, observing the events of last week, or seeing much of the life of the Church place by place, week by week – would anyone make the mistake of saying 'these people are full of new wine' (Acts 2:13)?

I owe to John Cairns the discovery of the tartan which I have been wearing occasionally this week. I thought it was called 'clergy tartan'. But I have learned that its proper name is 'muted clergy'! Not if I have anything to do with it!

A passionate Church – in a gentle Scotland. That is what we need – a gentle Scotland. It is one of the great triumphs of the Prince of Darkness that we have been tricked into despising gentleness and suspecting tenderness and growing up out of emotional sensitivity. I don't know how much of this is peculiarly Scottish; I don't know how much of it is peculiarly male. But it shouldn't be there.

A group of men was asked – I found this story in a book by Brian Wren – by its two women tutors to confront the difficulty they had in expressing warmth by telling others in the group what they liked about them. The request was met with silence, ten minutes of displacement activity, then an attack on the tutors for making such an absurd request – after all, they didn't really know each other. It took twenty-five minutes before one man turned to another and said 'I like you' – and this was in a course called 'Sexual Politics for Men'![1]

A gentle Scotland is what we need. A Scotland in which we can be tender to one another and affirm one another and belong to each other. In the words of a recent prime minister – a Scotland at ease with itself. Gentleness with each other, and gentleness with those who are different from us. Gentleness with children; gentleness with the old. Gentleness with refugees. Gentleness with our neighbours – did you know that one person in three has never spoken to his or her next-door neighbour?

A gentle Scotland. Certainly, the achieving of that will involve passion – how can Scotland be truly gentle when it remains the home of the nation's weapons of mass destruction? But the mistake is to postpone the gentleness anywhere until we have achieved it everywhere. Tenderness in building a community of shared values among very different people is not easy – but it is beyond price. Gentleness in our assessment of each other, gentleness in our treatment of each other. Gentleness with those for whom things have gone wrong. That is the spirit of Jesus. That is what Scotland needs. Tucked away at the end of the New Testament, the Letter of James has good advice for those who are to shape the community: 'Who is wise and understanding among you? Show by your good life that your works are done with gentleness born of wisdom' (James 3:13).

A passionate Church in a gentle Scotland. Three hundred years ago and more, Montrose lay at the head of King Charles' army in the forests of Rothiemurchus. 'In my dream,' he said, 'I saw all Scotland. A fair realm. All this goodly land. But doomed. Betrayed by a fatal disease. Every man a law unto himself. So that he will unite truly with none. It is our curse.'[2] Well, three centuries of a fatal disease is long enough. Now is the time to cure that disease and lift that curse. To learn that we belong together. That tenderness with each other is the only way.

Let us pray for a passionate Church in a gentle Scotland. For thus will we bring people near to God and let in the light.

Notes

1. See Brian Wren, *What Language Shall I Borrow?* (London: SCM Press, 1989), p. 17.
2. Nigel Tranter, *The Young Montrose* (London: Coronet, 1997), p. 339.

Sermons

For Occasions

Heaven is where you don't have to go to church
Remembering
What's new?
Hope in God
Burying two lies
Othniel
Don't quarrel about beef

Sunday Mornings

The marks of a dead church
What makes a congregation angry
What grows in the church garden?
Faithfulness is not enough
Our very own nativity play

FOR OCCASIONS

Heaven is where you don't have to go to church

THIS sermon was preached at the centenary of a church building.

John 2:19. Jesus answered them, 'Destroy this temple, and in three days I will raise it up'.

A friend of mine brought up in Glasgow's Govan defines heaven as 'where you can see Celtic play and lose every night'! Thomas More said that heaven was where there were no lawyers; but he was a lawyer himself and could get away with saying it. For one of the Bible writers, heaven was where there was no temple: in the vision of the Holy City in the Book of Revelation, it says: 'I saw no temple in the city' (Rev. 21:22). That means that, for the Bible, heaven is where you don't have to go to church!

That's this morning's thought: heaven is where you don't have to go to church. Sometimes you just *know* what that means. I remember coming out of church one Sunday with a professor of theology who muttered disgruntledly: 'Sunday between 11.00 and 12.00 is the longest hour of the week'! I have an old book called *Prayers for the Natural Man: The Kind of Prayers People Really Pray*.[1] There is a section called 'Prayers before worship'. 'O God, I hope the sermon doesn't last more than fifteen minutes.' 'Dear Lord, if I'd known he was preaching I'd have come to the early service.' Heaven is where you don't have to come to church.

If you are very devout, you might see that thought leading to a sermon about turning a duty into a privilege. Heaven is where you don't *have* to go to church. You don't have to go because you want to go. Maybe you are not there yet; but it is possible that you will grow more and more like the writer of the psalm who sang:

> *I joy'd when to the house of God*
> *Go up, they said to me.*

Ps. 122:1

I have known people who have said to me that their greatest pleasure was to go to church. They may have been telling the truth; and it is certainly very high-minded. But it is not what the Bible says when it says: 'I saw no temple in the city'. Heaven is where you don't go to church at all. What can that mean?

Heaven is where you don't have to go to *church*. Say it like that, and it brings you in touch with the Bible reading from St John which we read this morning. Jesus comes to cleanse the temple, and he is consumed with 'zeal for the house of God'. Maybe it is a story about the exploiters of the poor. Maybe it is a story about the trivialisation of the house of prayer. But, at the end of the story, there is a hint of something more radical and far-reaching. Jesus said: 'Destroy this temple, and in three days I will raise it again'. But the temple he was speaking of was his body. E P Sanders – some would say he is the leading New Testament scholar of the last thirty years – called that saying of Jesus the most important verse in the New Testament. And on this day and in this place, we are better placed than most to understand why.

Because today you are filled with love for this church. I hope you love this church. I know you love this church. I would think less of you if you did not love this church. But what you feel for this building is a tiny thing compared with what the temple in Jerusalem meant to any Jew. It was holy beyond anything we can imagine. You can get a hint of that in the news of a couple of months ago. Do you remember when Ariel Sharon marched up Temple Mount, marched up the very hill to the very spot where Jesus went that day? He brutally offended Islamic religion, he brought the Peace Process into dreadful peril, and he lit a fire that would burn throughout Jerusalem and Gaza and the West Bank and leave dozens of corpses in its wake. But what really offended orthodox Jews was none of that: what offended them was that he had gone on to the very holiest site, the temple site, improperly dressed and improperly cleansed. Its holiness and purity is that important, that special, that unique.

And Jesus comes to it and declares by word and deed: 'It won't last. It will be destroyed. And in me people will find what they seek in the Temple and its sacrifices. In me, in being close to me, listening to me and following me and trusting me, people will meet God. In my body will be made the sacrifice that the Temple was built for.'

In heaven, you won't have to go to church because there will be no need to. No temple, for the presence of God will be everywhere. Because Jesus will have won for us the joy and life and space and truth and thrill and beauty and peace and fun and adventure that being close to God might be for all and for always and for everywhere.

In heaven, you don't have to go to church. But for this morning, the thought is that in *heaven* you don't have to go to church. And this isn't heaven. The Bible puts it quite bluntly: 'God is in heaven and you are on earth' (Eccles. 5:2). It's no good pretending that the kingdom of God has come on earth and we know and feel the presence of God everywhere. For we don't: this is not

> *Where all we have willed or dreamed or hoped of good*
> *Shall exist.*[2]

In heaven, you don't have to go to church. But today, this

week, now, you are on earth. And I promise you that you have done the right thing this morning. This church – despite what Jesus said – is the right place to be today.

As it has been the right place to have been for the last 100 years. I take much pleasure in congratulating you on your centenary; I am very grateful for the privilege of taking part in this service. On earth, this church has been a place of hope and faith and love since 1900. I honour the service of faithful and gifted ministers, of musicians and artists of many kinds. Here, for a century, eager children have known that they are precious and accepted; tear-stained and lonely women have been assured that there is life beyond the grave; the armour of aggressive men has been pierced by the vulnerability of love. Here, the word of God has been preached for 5000 Sundays. Here, countless babies and some who were far from the pram have had the water of life splashed upon them and their names have been written in the Lamb's book of life. Here, the body of Christ broken for us has been shared in the unrepeatable holiness of the Lord's Supper. The history of this church is a history of sins forgiven and promises made and faith kept. I honour the story of this church; and I want you to be very proud this morning.

For even though in heaven you don't have to go to church, this is not heaven and you do have to go to church. You have to go to church if you want to stay believing when life is bitter and faith is hard; if you want to know that the story of freedom and love which is the story of Jesus is true and true for you; if you want to learn to touch the world with the compassion of Jesus; if you want to help to grow the tree of life whose leaves are for the healing of the nations. If you don't want your life to be shallow and selfish and materialist and ill at ease, then you have to go to church. This is the right place to be if you want to become the person God made you to be.

For the moment, you have to go to church. There are lots

of people for whom that may not be so; but for you, for now, you have to go to church. So make the most of it. Thrill to this morning's music; nourish the memories of days gone by; open your eyes to the particular beauties of this building; and walk away from it changed. Changed by being in church, changed into one who trusts God and forgives enemies and defends the poor and lives in peace. That is why, for the time being, you have to go to church. And why, for you, at least for now, this church is the place to be.

Notes
1. David Head, *Prayers for the Natural Man: The Kind of Prayers People Really Pray.*
2. From Robert Browning, 'Abt Vogler'.

Remembering

THIS sermon was preached at the Scottish National War Memorial.

A year or two ago, a stockbroker asked to see me. This was his problem. The Glasgow Stock Exchange was to be closed and the building knocked down. What were they to do with the war memorials housed there? He approached me because the memorials had been moved years ago from my parish. Would it be possible to find a home for them in our church? So we arranged a simple service, and now they have their place beside the war memorials of our congregation.

That is a typically Scottish way of remembering. Where more natural for war memorials to be placed than in a church? Remembering and *religion*. A very Scottish way of remembering, as shown by this service today. In a solemn place and on a solemn day for Scotland, it is understandable that even people who have little interest in religion feel that this today should be a religious service. I am proud to be here, and proud to be sharing this service with representatives of other Scottish churches. I hope the day is not far off when it will be possible to have representatives of other faiths here; for so we will reflect the identity of Scotland and the identity of our armed forces.

Remembering with religion. In prayer and hymn, holding before God those who have died. Allowing religion to open doors of meaning and depth and emotion which for most of us are kept pretty firmly locked most of the time. In other parts of the world there may be other ways of doing it, but in Scotland the way we know how to do it is to keep religion and remembering together.

But that is not enough. Learn from the sad, sad city of

Jerusalem that there are other things in remembering. In one terrible, beautiful spot there, you will learn remembering and *wretchedness*. There is a particular part of the Holocaust Museum which is called the Children's Museum. As you enter, you see the faces of children: large, black-and-white photographs of very ordinary-looking children; and you know who they are and your heart is very full. but you are not at all prepared for what is ahead. You move into a darkened hall, lit by tiny pin-prick lights. They tell you that there are a million and a half little lights, one for each dead child. You walk round the dark hall, unable to see any other light or any way out; and you hear the names of children read, one after another: their names and their ages and their homes. It does not take long for the horror, for the tragedy, for the wretchedness to overwhelm you; and no-one comes out the same person who went in.

I hope that remembrance services will always have the wretchedness of remembering in them. They must not become too pompous nor too grand nor too perfect. They must always have room for the dreadful human pain which lies behind the names. For the men and women and children whose bodies, minds and spirits were lost along with those who lost their lives. In Pat Barker's First World War novels, some of those being treated in Craiglockhart Hospital in Edinburgh for shell-shock find that they have developed a terrible speech impediment: the things they have suffered cannot be spoken of. Here, in our remembering, we do not do justice to the suffering of those who have gone before unless there is wretchedness in our remembering.

But that too is not enough. It is one of the most savage ironies of this generation, and a shocking illustration of the pervasive hold that evil has upon us all, that the very people who remember the wretchedness of the Second World War so movingly in Jerusalem are the very people who find themselves lapsing into racism and injustice themselves as they struggle to deal with Palestinian people. Remembering is not enough.

There must be remembering with *resolve*. So let me take you now to America. In the most famous speech ever made by an American – at least until Martin Luther King – Abraham Lincoln stood on a Civil War battlefield and combined remembering with resolve. His words are words we must not forget. He said:

> It is not for us to dedicate the memory of those who have fought and died. It is for us, the living, rather to be dedicated here to the great task remaining before us ... that we here highly resolve that the dead shall not have died in vain, that this nation under God shall have a new birth of freedom ...[1]

Our purpose here is not simply to remember: it is to resolve that we will be better men and women living in a better world.

Remembering with religion and wretchedness and resolve. Come now with me to France. The date of 30 April is different from all other days in the French Foreign Legion. It is the anniversary of the Battle of Cameron, the Legion's most glorious day. Sixty-three legionnaires were attacked by 2000 enemy soldiers and resisted until only five were left. These five then charged, and the three survivors passed on the tale. Every year since 1863, 30 April has been a day of celebration in the Foreign Legion. The troops are paraded and stand to attention while the story of the Battle of Cameron is read to them. Then the rest of the day is given over to rejoicing.

Remembrance with *rejoicing*. Are you offended by that? Or are you able to see that we truly honour those who have died for a future they never saw when we enter gladly and heartily and cheerfully into the peace and opportunity which have been given to us? Are you able to deal on one day only with wretchedness – or do you find within you a deeper humanity which can share both in the tears of things and also in the exuberant joyfulness which life can offer? What has been gained by those whom we remember here today is not a life of doleful and gloomy mourning. What they would want for us is a world in which children can play games and grown-ups can laugh and sing and feast. We diminish their sacrifice if we do not allow celebration and rejoicing to be part of our remembering. I have a hunch that it is those who, unlike me, know the reality of war who will be least prissy about this and most ready to enjoy the good that is ours. It is entirely appropriate to have a good and happy lunch today!

So to the one word which above all I want for our remembering today. Religion, wretchedness, resolve, rejoicing and *resurrection*. The truest remembering – certainly the truest Christian remembering – is remembering with resurrection. The single most important thing that can be said about dead people is that they are not dead to God. For some people here today, there will be a recent bereavement which is still fierce and sometimes overwhelming. I want to say to you that the person whom you have loved is not dead to God. Today we are remembering many, many thousands whose names we do not know. The mystery of Christian faith is that these ones too are alive to God.

I say that for two reasons. One is that I believe in the ultimate triumph of the love of God. Nothing is strong enough to defeat God. Somehow, God's loving purpose for each one of us will be fulfilled. So death is not strong enough to frustrate God's hopes for each of his children for ever. God will bring those whom he loves to healing and light. I say that confidently – and this is the other reason – because of Jesus Christ. In a garden, by a lake-shore, journeying on a road, the friends of Jesus came to know that death could not hold him and had not held him. And they proclaimed 'because he lives we shall live also'.

There is a vision of the city of God at the end of the Bible.

Its resurrection hope is the best way of remembering:

> The throne of God and of the Lamb shall be in it, and his servants will worship him. They will see his face and his name will be on their foreheads. And there will be no more night; they need no light of lamp or sun, for the Lord God will be their light, and they will reign for ever and ever. (Rev. 22:3–5)

Note

1. From Abraham Lincoln, *Address at Dedication of National Cemetery at Gettysburg*, 19 November 1863.

What's new?

THIS sermon was preached at the opening of a new church hall.

John 13:34. A new commandment I give to you, that you love one another.

I enjoy telling visitors to Scotland that I am minister of the New Town in Edinburgh and that means that my parish was laid out 250 years ago! There are seven golf courses in St Andrews; the second oldest is called the New Course! What was new once is old now. The new hall some day will need to be repainted.

When Jesus told his friends the commandment to love one another was a new commandment, perhaps that is the idea. New for them. But weary and familiar now. Perhaps the word 'new' in John 13:34 really now means 'old': exactly as New Town no longer means 'new'.

Except that Jesus must have been a fool if that is what he meant – or at least extraordinarily ignorant. For they had been quoting 'love your neighbour as yourself' from the old Book of Leviticus for hundreds of years before Jesus. And lots of other teachers had said similar things: the old rabbis took very seriously the idea of love, and there are plenty of sayings to prove it. So Jesus must have had a very bad memory if he called this commandment 'new' and he meant 'something you've not heard before'.

Perhaps he meant 'an old commandment with a new meaning'. The chapters of St John's gospel in which this new commandment is found are full of teaching about the relationship between the Father and the Son. That is the perfection of love, the model of love, the definition of love. And our love for one another is to be a reflection of that love, and a reflection of the love Jesus has for his friends. The Father loves the Son, the Son loves the disciples, and the disciples love one another. And their love is to be the same as the love of the Father for the Son and the love of the Son for the disciples.

That is a breathtaking thought. The love which you have to have for the people in this church is to be the love which we have seen in Jesus, who gave up his life for his friends. I suppose you could call that a new commandment. An old commandment with a new meaning. Jesus' 'new' commandment seems to speak quite specifically about the love the disciples are to have for one another. The new meaning might be the specific love of the followers of Jesus for one another. So Jesus' commandment is to make it clear that the distinguishing mark above all of his church is that we love one another.

I told the General Assembly this story. A while ago, an old man asked me for a lift into town. He had been at his bus stop for ages, and he was late and cold. As we chatted, he asked me how I had spent the day – it was a holiday Monday. I told him that I had driven all the way to visit a friend of mine in hospital in Inverness. 'Very good', said he. 'That's what I like to hear! I had a friend in England who was a bishop; but he never went near his neighbour when he was in hospital. That's professional Christians for you, whereas ordinary chaps like you, who probably never go near a church, are better Christians than the clergy types!'

There is a terrifying point to the story. What the world expects of Christians is that they love one another. What the world judges Christians on is that they love one another. And not just bishops, not just ministers – though the coldness of clerics is a terrible thing – but all of us, all of you. Of course, it is wretchedly unfair that this is how the world chooses to judge Christians – except that that is exactly what Jesus said. Jesus said that his commandment was that we love one another. Whatever you have done to gossip or to hurt or to belittle or to damage or to wound or to weaken or to cripple or to destroy any other member of the company of Christ, any other member of your congregation, any other who looked to you for love – whatever you have done to hurt the body of Christ is direct disobedience. Disobedience of Jesus Christ. Whose commandment is that we – we here – love one another.

The first explanation was that Jesus thought it was a new commandment. The second is that he thought it was an old commandment with a new meaning. The third is that Jesus was an existentialist philosopher! So he thought it was always a new commandment even though it had been said many times before. Every time the commandment to love one another is heard, it is being heard in a different situation by people who are different from what they were before. So although it is an old commandment, whenever it is heard in a new situation it is as if it is being heard for the first time. In every different situation, people who are different are hearing a new commandment: and that means it is as if they are hearing the commandment for the first time. It becomes a new commandment.

The film *Dead Poets' Society* is the story of an English teacher who meets the least interested, most disaffected class in the school. To teach them English has defeated his predecessors. Shakespeare, Keats, Wordsworth – they've heard it all before. Except they haven't heard it all before. The genius of his teaching is that he allows them to hear for the first time what they have heard dozens of times before. All of a sudden, the power and beauty and thrill of the poetry comes alive for them. Although it is the twentieth time they have heard the words, it is the first time they have heard them. The poetry is new for them. It may be the 400th time you have heard the commandment of Jesus to love one another. But you need to hear it anew.

And this new hall. This new hall may some day grow old,

though it will still be called 'the new hall' when the paint is peeling. But it will be a new hall. It will still be the new hall every time it shows forth the commandment of Jesus, the commandment that you love one another. Every time some child, fresh and innocent and excited, hears here that she is precious to God and needed by God; every time that some child tear-stained and frightened and hurt knows here that he is loved and healed and belongs; every time this hall gives space to the commandment of Jesus that you love one another, then the hall is new again and the commandment is new again. Every time here old people find that they are not forgotten but remembered, not useless but useful, not only receivers but also givers, then the commandment of Jesus is made new. Every time from this hall the people of this community discover the energy and the healing and the mission of the church of Christ, the welcome and the judgement and the hope of the church of Christ; every time this city and the whole created world receive from this hall the justice and the peace of God, then, every time, the commandment of Jesus that you love one another is made new and this hall deserves its proud title the 'new hall'. For it is a title which will mean that the commandment of Jesus that you love one another is being obeyed and made new among you.

Or maybe Jesus simply meant this. A new commandment is like a new suit. I have a suit in my wardrobe which has been there for twelve months and I have never worn it. I have never worn it because it is my new suit and I feel I must keep it good. So it is still my new suit; but it has been no use to me whatever. A new commandment in that sense, perhaps? G K Chesterton remarked that the thing is not that Christianity has been tried and found wanting. It is that it has not been tried.

Hope in God

THIS sermon was preached at the anniversary of a congregation worshipping in a community hall.

Romans 8:24. In hope we were saved.

Hope in God. That is the motto of some ancient Scottish clan; and an aunt of mine had the name of that clan. So one day she made an expedition to visit the old family seat of the clan chief. She was delighted to see the family motto in huge letters above the front door. Except that one letter had fallen off: so instead of 'Hope in God' above the door, it read 'Hop in God'!

Since by our prayers and our hymns we have already invited God to be with us here in the Community Centre this morning, and since God was here before us anyway and will be here after we leave, I don't feel any need to exclaim 'Hop in God' this morning. But 'Hope in God' – now that's a different matter. Easier said than done! It says in the Bible 'In hope we were saved … If we hope for what we do not see, we wait for it with patience' (Rom. 8:25). Do we really?

You need to use your whole body if you're going to learn to hope. First, you need to learn to hope with your *head*. Hoping includes thinking. One of the marvellous things about being Moderator is that I get to meet all sorts of remarkable people; and last week I met the man with the worst job in the world. I had an hour alone with Sir Ronnie Flanagan, the Chief Constable of the RUC. We talked about the Peace Process and about the Patten Report on policing in Northern Ireland, and I asked him what his mood was just now. 'You have to distinguish between optimism and hope', he said. 'There are optimistic people and pessimistic people: but that is just a matter of personality. But hope – now hope is based on the evidence.

You have to look at what is going on and what is not going on: you have to interpret the signs around you; you have to think. And only then can you begin to hope – once you have got some evidence to support your hope.'

Hope with your head. Did you hear the news about superbugs? These tiny monsters which live in our hospitals and develop unbelievably subtle and successful defences against the most powerful antibiotics? Well, last week a scientist in the Western General Hospital in Edinburgh, which is just round the corner from where I live, announced that he had considerable scientific evidence that the superbugs were on the run, and the day might be coming when they would be annihilated. 'We've done the experiments and we've shown the research, and now is the time to hope that the days of these killers are numbered.' Since then, new alarming evidence has unfortunately suggested that more thinking may need to be done before hope can clearly be based on science on this issue.

Hope with your head. It is very Christian to use your brains to help you to hope. To look at the evidence which supports hoping in God. The evidence of science, of the Bible, of history, of philosophy. The evidence of the lives of people you know; the evidence of moments in your own life when you have been helped and held and healed. The evidence of the unconquerable power of love, the unmatched power of love to change things and to change things for good. It is sheer nonsense to dismiss hoping in God as wishful thinking, as living in fairyland, as storybook stuff. Hope in God because the evidence you have been looking at all your life makes that a wise and sensible and level-headed thing for a thinking person to do.

You need to use your whole body to hope properly. You need to learn to hope with your *hands*. Hoping is not just about how you feel inside. Hoping is about what you do. In the Bible, Jeremiah bought a piece of land. He was laughed at for doing it – they all said that it was the worst time and the worst place to buy land: the whole country was going to the dogs. But Jeremiah hoped in God, and hoped that God's good day would come. And to make his hope real, he bought a piece of land. It was as if he were investing in the future. He was refusing to give in. He was putting his money where his hope was.

Forty years ago in this place, they hoped and they hoped with their hands. It wasn't just pious words: it was doing and making and building. So forty years ago, this congregation began. Forty years ago, this part of Scotland was not always an easy place to live in and not always an easy place to be a Christian in and not always an easy place to have hope in. So we come today to honour those who had hope then. To recognise the hope of the different authorities, church authorities and public authorities, who made this possible. To honour the hope of Christian people from this town who committed themselves from the start to the project, to its work and its worship, and to praying for the Christian community here. But most of all, we are here to honour those who have been here from the start over forty years to this present day, to those people who live here for whom this has been the House of God and the Sunday community and the object of their love and their efforts and their costly discipleship. And we are here to honour God who has blessed this struggling, beautiful, fragile, precious part of the building of his kingdom for forty years.

What is that if not hoping with your hands? Hoping with the hands that have worked and cuddled and held wounded people and prayed and gathered money and produced music and cleaned up – and done it all for God?

You need your whole body for hoping: most of all, you need your *heart*. Hoping with your heart is what believing is.

Hoping is about thinking and it is about doing; but most of all, it is about believing. So this morning, most of all I want you to hope with your heart. This morning, as we peer into the future and do not know what we see. As we peer into the future of worship here and the future of this town. As we peer into the future of the Church and of Christian faith in Scotland. As we – each of us – peer ahead to what lies ahead in our own lives and do not know what we see. This morning, I invite you to hope with all your heart.

When the enemy is despair, hope in God. When it looks as if all your best efforts count for nothing, as if the family home you hoped to build has been torn apart, when there is the unremitting grind of trying to keep going when you don't have enough money to keep going week after week, year after year, when the sickness never leaves you, then remember God. The writer of one of the psalms said: 'Look to him and be radiant. This poor soul cried and was heard by the Lord' (Ps. 34:5–6).

When it is fear that destroys you, then hope in God. It may be that there is a particular person who makes you really afraid; or it may be a general numbing anxiety which spoils all your life. It may be that you have lived with fear all your days; or it may be that old age has brought terror with it. Some are frightened to be alone; some are frightened of violence, some are frightened of dying. When fear is the enemy – and a very strong enemy it is – then hope in God. When one Bible character was beginning the great enterprise of his life, he heard words from God which might help you to hope: 'Be strong and courageous; do not be frightened or dismayed, for the Lord your God is with you wherever you go' (Josh. 1:9).

Hope with your heart and with your hands and with your head. And you may become a little like the best example of hope I know apart from Jesus himself. Here is a little story of St Francis to send you away from here in the right mood. At the great crisis of his life, he had quarrelled with his father and given up the wealth and position which he might have had. He went out into the cold world.

He went half-naked into the winter woods, walking the frozen ground between the frosty trees: a man without a father. He was penniless, he was parentless, he was to all appearance without a trade or a plan or a hope in the world; and as he went under the frosty trees, he burst suddenly into song.[1]

Note

1. G K Chesterton, *St Francis of Assisi* (London: Hodder & Stoughton, n.d.), p. 62.

Burying two lies

THIS sermon was preached in St Mary's Roman Catholic Cathedral, Edinburgh, at the opening of the Edinburgh Festival.

It is a great honour to be the first Moderator of the General Assembly to be invited to preach in St Mary's Cathedral; but I am just as pleased to come here this morning as your parish minister! My text is in the gospel according to St John:

John 8:44. The devil is a liar and the father of lies.

Maybe he is, but no lie can live for ever. Thomas Carlyle was right: no lie can live for ever.[1] I am here this morning to bury two lies which are dead and should have been pronounced such long ago.

It is a lie that Protestants are against Catholics. It is a lie which has done immense damage to Protestants, for it has allowed the most wicked parts of our psychology – I mean our capacity to hate people – to have some spurious quasi-religious justification. Protestants have been much damaged by being told that it is all right to hate Catholics. And it is a lie which has done much damage to Catholics. Anyone who knows how heavy industry used to work in Scotland – shipbuilding is the example I know best – knows that for generations promotion was out of the question if you went to a school called St Anything's.

It is a lie which has hurt Scotland, but it is a lie. Protestants are not against Catholics. It is not true on a personal level. In this place, I am pleased to call Father David Gemmell and Archbishop Keith O'Brien my friends. I am proud of the support Irene has received as Moderator's wife from the Catholic school in which she teaches.

43

It is not true on an institutional level. The Church of Scotland is not against Catholics. The highest authority in our church is the General Assembly, so let me tell you of two precious moments in our General Assembly in which I had some part. About fifteen years ago, an elder in the congregation of which I was minister, and a dear friend of mine, changed the law of the Church of Scotland. He was no longer prepared to have anything to do with a Confession of Faith which spoke of the Roman Catholic Church in the violent terms of the battles of three and four centuries ago. So, single-handedly, he persuaded the General Assembly to pass an act stating that the anti-Catholic statements of the Westminster Confession were not part of the substance of the faith of the Church of Scotland.

And this year, the high point of the General Assembly was the address by a Canadian Roman Catholic called Jean Vanier. He is the founder of L'Arche, communities of people with learning difficulties and their assistants. He spoke wonderfully about handicap and weakness and Jesus and the gospel, and everyone in our Assembly knew that we were hearing God speaking to us from the lips of a Roman Catholic. It is not true that Protestants are against Catholics.

Of course, we don't agree with Catholics about everything; if we did, then you would all be Protestants! It is a matter of great hurt to us that we are not able to share in Christian sacraments with our Catholic sisters and brothers; and we disagree strongly about what the Bible means about justice for women and the ordination of women. We recognise that you are upset by much that we believe about ethical questions about birth and death and sexuality. But these things do not mean – and must not mean – that we are against each other. Catholics and Protestants are together in their faith in God as Father, Son and Holy Spirit. Catholics and Protestants are together in the struggle for justice for the poor and peace in the world and in the struggle for personal holiness and gentleness and depth. Most of all, Protestants and Catholics together live under the clear and inescapable words of the Bible:

> Those who say 'I love God' and hate their brothers and sisters are liars; for those who do not love a brother or sister whom they have seen cannot love God whom they have not seen. The commandment we have from him is this: those who love God must love their brothers and sisters also. (1 John 4:20–1)

There is no other way. That is how it is for Protestants and for Catholics. Those who say that Protestants are against Catholics are liars. But no lie can live for ever, and this one is long past its die-by date.

Interestingly, it was in the context of the Edinburgh Festival that these matters last came under public discussion. James McMillan created quite a storm when he blamed the difficulties of creating great art in Scotland today on a kind of Philistinism of Protestantism. The storm which greeted his remarks suggested that there were other ways of looking at Scotland: if I am right, then anti-Catholic prejudice among us is increasingly a thing of the past. But the debate which followed his remarks grew into another big lie. For there were those who took the opportunity to say again what has often been said before: that not only Protestantism but Christianity itself is against the arts. And that is the other big lie which I want to bury this morning. The lie that Christians are against the arts.

That is not true. It was never as true in Scotland as the enemies of Christianity like to claim. Even what are called the dark days of post-Reformation Scotland were a great deal more artistic and creative than ignorant people usually suggest. It was after the Reformation that the tradition of domestic Biblical painting in Scotland began, that poetry flourished, and that Scottish church music was reborn. Protestantism has been a friend to the arts in Scotland – as has Catholicism. How could anyone walk into the church building which I know best, St Andrew's and St George's, a few hundred yards from here, and look for two minutes round that beautiful little masterpiece of art and still think of Scottish Christians as Philistines? It is not true that Christians are against the arts.

It is a lie which you always hear at Festival time. The only Christian comment you are likely to read in the press about the Festival will be some unhappy whine about falling standards of sexual morality. And all the time the sensitive, intelligent, generous support of the Festival by Christian people and by the churches goes unremarked. Were the churches of Edinburgh to withdraw their committed support for the arts in this week, the Festival – and in particular the Fringe – would look very different. I would like to think that this goes unremarked because it is the natural way that people expect Christians to behave; but I fear that the lie that Christians are against the arts is taking a long time to die.

Not just at Festival time. Think of all the wonderful music that is made within a mile from this building Sunday after Sunday after Sunday. Think of the hymn-writing of contemporary Scotland which is enriching the church all over the world. Last month, I had the delight of receiving a beautiful new silver cross commissioned by the Church of Scotland for the Millennium; and I am very pleased that the student at the Glasgow School of Art whose design won the prize is a Roman Catholic. It is not true that Christianity is against the arts.

How could it be true when Christians believe that God is most God when he is creating? That creation is the very heart of who God is and what God does. When we create something lovely and lasting – or even when we create something fun – we are coming very close to the true nature of God.

How could it be true that Christianity is against the arts when both are seeking to explore the meaning of life? Both are attempting to give shape and understanding to the glory and the pain which is what it means to be human. Whenever I have the opportunity to talk to preachers about preaching, I like to suggest that if they only read one book it should be *King Lear*. For we preachers will learn far more from that play about life and mystery and pain and God and faith than from any work of theology. And what is preaching about if it is not about life and mystery and pain and God and faith? It is in the great, terrible, wonderful masterpieces of art that we learn who we are. And that is how we learn who God is and how God is with us.

It is a lie that Christianity is against the arts. Great art wrestles with the same questions, struggles with the same fears, shows us the darkness and points us to the light. When much of church life is trivial and commonplace and self-centred, thank God for Shakespeare and van Gogh and James McMillan. The more depth the more truth; the more truth the more God. Let Christianity embrace our partner in the human endeavour. How could Christianity be the enemy of art?

No-one ever accused St Paul of a life of heedless pleasure-seeking. So, when he writes of beauty and of loveliness as the keys to the heart of God, he is worth listening to: 'Whatever is true, whatever is honourable, whatever is just, whatever is pure, whatever is pleasing, whatever is commendable, if there is any excellence and if there is anything worthy of praise, think about these things' (Phil. 4:8).

It might be that the most Christian thing you could do all this week would be to go to a concert.

Note

1. See Thomas Carlyle, *The French Revolution* (first published 1837), vol. 1, book 3.

Othniel

THIS sermon was preached after the death of the First Minister, Donald Dewar.

Judges 3:9. The Lord raised up a deliverer for the Israelites who delivered them, Othniel son of Kenaz.

Why choose the story of Othniel son of Kenaz? For he was the first First Minister under a new constitution, and he was the ideal and faithful leader. The Bible says of him: 'The spirit of the Lord came upon him, and he led Israel ... So the land had peace for forty years' (Judg. 3:10–11).

So Othniel is the obvious choice for today. Well, perhaps not obvious, since before writing this sermon I don't remember ever seeing his name! But an easy way in to say a word about Donald Dewar. Like Othniel, he was the first First Minister under a new constitution. He wasn't the ideal or faithful leader – though I suspect that years from now, the same rose-coloured memories which wrote the story of Othniel will write the story of Donald Dewar. Not perfect – but he was great.

'Cometh the hour, cometh the man.' Donald Dewar was the right person in the right place at the right time, and he will never quite be replaced. He was a politician with all the capacity for compromise and dealing that that implies. But he was a politician whose principles have raised up the rest of Scottish public life, and whose transparent wholesomeness suggests that he was born to be Scotland's first First Minister.

It's easy to see why I chose Othniel today. It's not quite so easy to see why he is in the Bible. Indeed, why are all these chaps in the Bible? The Book of Judges is full of stories of people like Othniel – or people not like Othniel, because most of them are pretty deficient. There's Samson and Deborah and

Jephthah and some others, none of whom managed to get it all right. Othniel is the best of the bunch. But there's no mention of any of them going to church or reading the Bible or giving away their money or being faithful wives and husbands or being kind to the poor. So why are they in the Bible? The answer to that question is the single most important lesson anyone has to learn in reading the Bible. It is that the Bible believes that it is in the things that happen in the world that we are to find and meet and learn about God. If the Bible is right, where God is most at work and most to be found is in the stories of people like Othniel, in the stories of people who made laws and fought armies and established nations and raised taxes and brought people out of slavery into freedom.

We get it wrong when we place God mostly inside ourselves. Ask any modern person where God is to be found, and the answers will be 'in church' or 'in your conscience' or 'in feeling peaceful' or 'in praying'. Ask any Bible person where God is to be found, and the answer will be in the story, the history, the politics of people like Othniel, or David, or Moses; or – especially and most of all – in the story of Jesus. The story of Jesus living in Roman occupation under a puppet king. The story of Jesus weeping over Jerusalem. The story of Jesus crucified by the government of the day.

A year ago, the press all quoted me saying that I wanted to be a 'political' Moderator. What I meant by that – whatever they meant – was that I wanted to be a Biblical Moderator, finding God in the story of what happens in the world.

Which brings me, this week, back to Donald Dewar. Let me suggest how the Bible might have thought about the death of Donald Dewar, how we might think about his death as we seek to believe in God.

It might be possible to see the hand of God in the life and death of Donald Dewar in building a new Scotland. After all, that is precisely what the Bible says about Othniel: it is why he is remembered and why he is in the Bible. He set about shaping the people, stragglers from the desert journeys, into a nation; and that, for the Bible, is the work of God. Our late First Minister was not Othniel, but the building of a nation, working out what it is that will hold people together, creating a fairer society, making laws that are just and honourable – it is in these things that the Bible wants us to see God at work. In the politics of our nation, in making Scotland what she is meant to be – that is where we are to look for God.

We will all have different views on the success of the Scottish parliament and the government of the last year and a half; but there is only one Christian view about the importance of the political endeavour. Christian faith is based, said one of my old professors, on what God is doing in the world to make and to keep human life human.

Or it might be possible to seek faith in God in the sadness and loss and bereavement we have all felt this week. A woman said to me: 'I never met Donald Dewar, but he has been my friend for twenty years'. It goes far beyond the personal. There is the general recognition that death has with one blow thrown our people into a fragile and difficult and unhappy time: for we are by no means sure what lies ahead for us now, and where Scotland will be going. Christian faith is made for times like these. For it is in all the uncertainties and frailties and inadequacies of the history of God's people in Israel, all the inadequate people and self-seeking people who followed Othniel as rulers, in all the wicked stories of vulnerable King David and his like – it is in these places and in these stories that the people of the Bible confirmed and strengthened and established their faith in God. Their faith in God who is stronger than death and whose love will never leave them and who is already at work for the sake of all our tomorrows. John Calvin used to say that Geneva was ruled in the confusion of men and the providence of God. So was Israel; and so will Scotland be.

It is that same hope which we need to bring to the other terrible news of this week: the news of how near war is in the Middle East. In our gospel reading, Jesus wept over Jerusalem; who would not weep for Jerusalem today? The old rabbis used to say: 'Ten measures of beauty gave God to the world; nine to Jerusalem and one to the remainder. Ten measures of sorrow gave God to the world: nine to Jerusalem and one to the remainder.'[1]

I don't claim to understand the Middle East. But there are some things we can say. We can say that Britain has a special responsibility, since it was the terms of the ending of our Mandate which created the modern state of Israel. We can say that the presence of Church of Scotland staff in Israel and Palestine – ours is the only British church with congregations there – gives us a special responsibility. We can say that memories of the Holocaust must always be a powerful factor in European concern for Jewish people; but that concern for Jewish people is by no means the same as support for the Israeli government. We can say that Palestinian people have been treated with great injustice. We can say that resolutions of the United Nations must count for as much in Israel as they do in Iraq. But today the only appropriate reaction is to weep.

And to look for God. That's what the Bible wants us to do. That's why Othniel is in the Bible. That's what we tried to do with the death of Donald Dewar. To look for God in the things that happen. In the politics and the history going on around us. So in the Middle East that means we are to look for God in the tireless efforts of those who are even at this moment working for peace. To look for God in the certainty that peace without justice is never ever peace for long. To look for God in the brave and gentle spirits in both Palestinian and Jewish communities who have not been made bitter and despairing by the conflict. To look for God in the prayers of wretched souls in that land and all over the world. To look for God in the concentration in Jerusalem of three great religions and in the determination of God to overcome the dangers of religion for the sake of the healing of religion.

Most of all, the people of the Bible are to look for God in one place and in one way. To look for God in the history of Jerusalem where Jesus was crucified and rose again that all the world might believe that no death is strong enough, no horror is black enough, no darkness is cruel enough to defy for ever the power of God, whose only name is love and whose will shall be done in Jerusalem and in Scotland and in all the created universe.

Note
1. From the Jewish Talmud.

Don't quarrel about beef

THIS sermon was preached at the Houses of Parliament.

I start with the quarrel about beef – indeed, with two quarrels about beef. One is in the Old Testament and one in the New Testament. The New Testament one is the elder brother's bad temper over his father's decision to provide choice steak from the fatted calf to celebrate the return of the prodigal son. The Old Testament one is Jacob and Esau. Their old father is about to die, and Esau sees himself diddled out of the inheritance that is rightly his by a cheap trick Jacob pulls with a rich, tasty casserole.

From these two quarrels over beef, I want to say two things to you this morning which are so obvious as to be almost embarrassingly simple. But I suspect that even very sophisticated politicians are often simple human beings who need to hear and hear again what we all know.

First, don't quarrel. It isn't worth it. Invariably, the happiest people I know are those who carry with them the fewest quarrels; the most useful people are those who don't spend their time conspiring; and the best people are those who don't allow themselves to be eaten up with trying to get even. I don't know whether or not politicians are more prone to quarrelling than the rest of us – well yes, I do; because history suggests that no-one is more likely to be quarrelsome than a quarrelsome clergyman. So from bitter personal experience and from the experience of twenty centuries of church history, I beg you – don't quarrel.

Of course, you must argue and rage and dispute and defeat your opponents – that is what you are paid for. But don't quarrel. It isn't worth it. It wasn't worth it for Jacob and Esau. From the row with the stew (really goat stew rather than beef stew) came years and years of pain: pain to themselves and to their families and to their whole people. You cannot measure the cost of a quarrel – prevention is always better than cure. The story Jesus told about the two brothers ends with the quarrel just beginning. Who knows whether the elder brother went to the party and enjoyed himself or stayed outside and sulked and nursed a grievance and plotted revenge? Who knows? But you know which is better.

Two things about both of these quarrels. Did you spot that both of them are quarrels between brothers? Isn't that so poignant? How often it is easier to love those outside your own family, your own party, your own church, your own nation. It was wonderfully moving for me on Tuesday to be received with the warmest reception I have encountered since I became Moderator: the occasion was my presence at the 400th anniversary of the Scots Catholic College in Rome. And even that tiny sign of the healing of ancient quarrels was very important for both sister churches.

And did you notice that both of the quarrels, Jacob and Esau in the Old Testament and the prodigal son and his brother in the New, were really quarrels caused by jealousy? If we could learn to recognise jealousy when we see it, to call it by its name and to stamp on it and destroy it – I mean if we could destroy jealousy in ourselves – then we would find quarrels a great deal more easy to avoid. There was an old desert monk in the early days of Christianity. A junior devil was trying to tempt him into sin. He spoke to him of wealth and luxury; but the old hermit stood firm. He showed him visions of voluptuous women; but the old hermit stood firm. The junior devil reported back to his commander-in-chief that the task was hopeless, the monk was firmly established in goodness. The arch-tempter himself slithered out to the desert and up to the monk and whispered in his ear: 'Did you hear that your brother has just been made Bishop of Alexandria?' and at once the purple veins were standing out on the hermit's neck and the old master had another conquest.

Don't quarrel. How? How to avoid it? It's the most natural thing in the world. Which brings me to the second thing I want to say about the two Bible stories about beef quarrels. They are both stories about depth. The way to avoid quarrelsomeness is to avoid shallowness. The second thing I want to say this morning is 'go deep'.

In this morning's paper, I read about the actress Alicia Silverstone who has just been awarded the Plain English Campaign award for 'The Most Baffling Statement of the Year' when she was talking about exactly the same thing. I think! She said about her part in the film *Clueless*: 'I think *Clueless* was very deep. I think it was very deep in the way that it was very light. I think lightness has to come from a very deep place if it is true lightness'! I hope I can be a little less dialectical when I plead this morning for depth. Go deep.

There's a book by Monica Furlong called *Travelling in*: she says that the religious person thinks that life is about making some kind of journey; the non-religious person thinks that there is no journey to make. In that sense, I am a religious person, and I believe that a vital part of the journey is to journey deep.

It's in the other story about Esau which we read that you see it most clearly: the story of selling his birthright for a mess of pottage. Esau cared about stew; Jacob cared about birthright and family and tradition and religion and future hopes. Jacob is by no means a good person, but he cares about deep things and feels about deep things – although at this stage in his life he merely tries to turn them to his advantage. Try to imagine Esau's world-view, try to put words into his mouth about the things in his life that have been really important, about the mysteries and the sweetness of life – and you don't come up with much. Of course you sympathise with Esau, but he is a shallow, shallow man.

Just like the prodigal's elder brother. Of course you sympathise with him, but there is nothing in him of wonder or forgiveness or healing: it's all about keeping the score and not letting anyone get away with anything and getting even. He is a blinkered, jealous, shallow man – and I hope so much that he changed his mind and came to the party. Go deep.

William McIlvanney wrote an essay a few years ago called 'The shallowing of Scotland'. It was about our political life and the absence of idealism, about our cultural life and 'dumbing down', about our personal lives and the way we cut ourselves off from each other. In the years since he used the word, despite the achievements of our parliament, the shallowing of Scotland has not slowed up.

To make the journey inside yourself is what you need. What we need – what the world needs – is deep people. That is what we need most in our political leaders – deep people. Onward and upward is all very well in its way; but left to itself it leads to aggression and competitiveness and disappointment and insecurity and quarrels. Downward and inward: that is what we need. If we are to grow, we need to deepen our roots. If we are to break our devotion to the false values which drive us and drive us, we need to go down and down to the best, to the richest, to the most creative things we know – deep into love and justice and truth. This isn't about being a real politician – it's about being a real human being. And that is the best way, the only way, of being a real politician.

At the General Assembly this year, I had the honour to introduce to the Assembly one of the true religious leaders of the world, Jean Vanier. Jean Vanier founded the L'Arche communities, communities all over the world for people with severe learning difficulties and for their assistants. Once in Bangladesh, at a conference for parents, a man got up to speak. 'My name is Dominique', he said. 'I have a son,

Vincent, who has a severe handicap. He was a beautiful child when he was born, but at six months he had a terribly high fever which brought on convulsions. It affected his brain and his nervous system. Now, at sixteen, he has severe damage. He cannot walk or talk or eat by himself. He is completely dependent. He cannot communicate, except through touch. My wife and I suffered a lot. We prayed to God to heal our Vincent. And God answered our prayer, but not in the way that we expected. He has not healed Vincent, but he has changed our hearts. He has filled my wife and myself with joy at having a son like him.' Jean Vanier went on: 'Reality is not always changed. But by a gift of God, our barriers and preconceived ideas fall, doors are opened within us. A new strength surges up permitting us not only to accept reality but to live it peacefully and even to love it.'[1]

Go deep. Go deep and you will meet yourself. Go deep and you will meet God. Go deep and God will give you the gift of loving what you find.

Note

1. Jean Vanier, *Our Journey Home* (London: Hodder & Stoughton, 1997), p. 166.

SUNDAY MORNINGS

The marks of a dead church

Matthew 2:1–12. The chief priests and the scribes.

I NEVER thought of them before. There they are in a story I've read countless times and preached on for thirty years. Yet I never really thought of them before. I wonder why.

There they are in the middle of the story of the wise men. Our Bible calls them 'the chief priests and the scribes'. They are the religion of their day; the leaders of religion. They are as near as first-century Judaism gets to the Church. They are as near as it gets to Moderators. And they bear the marks of a dead church.

Mark one is *religion without faith*. They have the scriptures at their command. They can deal with the theological question which the wise men and Herod put to them. But it doesn't mean anything to them; it makes no difference to their lives. They don't care about faith, they don't care about God, they don't care about the purpose of their lives. What they care about is religion; and religion without faith spells death.

How else can you explain it? The heart of their religion in the time of the New Testament was watching, waiting, expecting. Watching for the moment when God would visit his people and claim them for his own. That is what they believed, what they taught, what they prayed about. The coming of the Messiah. And when news comes that a birth nearby may be the very fulfilment of their expectation, their weary, supercilious response is: 'Oh well, if you're really interested, here's the information you might need'. It beggars belief! An opportunity to be at the very centre of God's great new day – and they can't be bothered paying much attention! You could understand it if they greeted the wise men with wild enthusiasm; you could understand it if they greeted the wise men with violent hostility and suspicion – perhaps they were about to start a rival cult. But their reaction is neither. Their reaction is 'Please don't disturb our routine. Leave us to get on with the rituals and the studies and the traditions which we love; but please don't bring God into it all. Please don't ask us to believe too much of all this stuff!' Plenty of religion, but no faith.

Can you recognise that? Would you recognise a church that had religion without faith? A church that was only interested in religion would give emphasis to what goes on inside its members, to what it calls experience and good feelings and even spirituality: all sorts of ways of being interested in ourselves and our souls and bodies and what we do. A church that lives by faith, on the other hand, is turned towards God and God's will and God's holiness. A church that is full of religion but empty of faith will tell that the gospel is to do with doing our best and doing our best for God – while a church that lives by faith will ask for forgiveness and walk cheerfully in the mercy of God. Religion means doing the old things in the comfortable spirit of well-loved routine. Faith means taking the risk that God is real and alive and at work in the world and in the church.

These chief priests and scribes knew which side their bread was buttered on. It wasn't easy to flourish under King Herod. Indeed, it wasn't easy to survive under King Herod. An unprincipled, vindictive tyrant as he was, the only thing more dangerous than being one of his friends was being one of his family. Wives, sons, nephews – none was safe from his ruthless destruction of those he feared might be his enemies. But the chief priests and scribes survived. There they are in our story at the beck and call of the great king, dancing to his bidding. How did they survive? By displaying one of the marks of a dead church. They chose the side of the rich and powerful. A dead church is marked by cosying up to those whom the world counts great. By choosing *respectability without righteousness*. The direct consequence of their fawning advice to Herod was the slaughter of the innocents – the death of the helpless children of Judaea. And the scriptures record from them not one squeak of protest at that terrible act. They knew on which side their bread was buttered.

Church history bristles with examples of this fatal preference of the Church. This fatal desire to choose life with the rich and powerful rather than life on the side of the oppressed. This fatal desire to be seen to count in society. Church history shows that national churches are particularly prone to this wrong choice: their pattern is in the national established religion of the chief priests and scribes in our story. The classic example is in Germany in the 1930s. Nearly every church, nearly every minister thought that it was better to stay on good terms with Hitler than to remain faithful to Christ. When the Nazis asked every theological faculty in Germany whether the New Testament supported their ban on Christians of Jewish extraction becoming ministers in the Church – a question, you might think, about which there can be absolutely no argument – of twenty-seven professors consulted, only the great Rudolph Bultmann dared to defy the regime and state what the Bible plainly teaches. Everyone else thought it was better to give Hitler the answer he wanted. Everyone thought it was better to give Herod the answer he wanted. Respectability without righteousness. A church like that is dead.

The story of the Church of Scotland is not one of which we can be universally proud. Our church's record at the time of the Highland Clearances is one of habitual collusion with the rich and powerful in their pursuit of profit at the expense of people. So let us be resolute today that a church which does not side with the oppressed – wherever they are to be found – bears the marks of death. In South America in this generation, a dead church has become a living church by rediscovering this principle. In Scotland, let a living church never prefer respectability to righteousness. The words of the hymn may be old-fashioned, but the spirit is right:

> *Set our feet on lofty places, gird our lives*
>   *that they may be*
> *Armoured with all Christ-like graces*
>   *in the fight to set men free,*
> *Grant us wisdom, grant us courage,*
>   *that we fail not men nor thee.*[1]

The scribes and Pharisees at Herod's court – the marks of a dead church. How else could you describe a church that asks no questions. When the wise men come with this astonishing suggestion, they talk but they do not listen; they pronounce but they do not try to understand. They answer but they do not ask – they do not ask anything! The mark of a dead church – *answers without questions.*

I've been having an interesting time recently with a probationer minister. For he has been reading a book by a radical Cambridge theologian called Don Cupitt. And in just over 100 pages, Cupitt has put a whole range of questions about faith and God and evil and religion and hope which the probationer had hardly encountered before. Theological training, Cupitt says in a fine phrase, prevents people from asking the questions that everyone asks, because divinity students are 'inoculated against any infection from this quarter'![2] If Cupitt is right, and we train our ministers not to ask questions, then we bear the marks of a dead church.

You might find it interesting sometime to go through your Bible to note the questions Jesus asked. You would find that some of the most important things he said were questions. You could read the Old Testament in search of the questions which

God asks his people. You might reflect on the words of Jesus about becoming like a little child and wonder if it is in the asking of questions that you might find a way to do that.

When Galileo's science brought the new questions to the Church, the Church was scared of the questions and nearly lost the soul of Europe. When Darwin's science brought the new questions to the Church, the Church was scared of the questions and nearly lost the soul of Europe. In our day, when genetics and information technology and space research and nuclear physics and psychology are bringing the new questions to the Church, again the soul of Europe is at stake. A church which asks questions, which shares in questions, which dares to admit that there are things we do not know – that church will live. But a church that has all the answers and no questions – that bears the marks of a dead church.

There they are in the story of the wise men, the scribes and the Pharisees. Now I know why I never noticed them before: because they bear the marks of a dead church. Religion without faith, respectability without righteousness, answers without questions. A few years ago, a senior police officer was telling me about an experiment in a troubled area of a great city which was involving all elements of the community. 'I've brought together', she told me, 'tenants' associations and public agencies and parents' groups and GPs and social workers – everyone who might have something to say.' Tentatively, I asked: 'What about the local churches?' She looked blank for a moment; then she murmured: 'It never occurred to me that they would have anything to contribute'. Just like in the Bible story – no-one notices a dead church.

Notes
1. From CH3 88.
2. Don Cupitt, *After All* (London: SCM Press, 1994), p. 17.

What makes a congregation angry

Luke 4:28. These words roused the whole congregation to fury; they leapt up, drove him out of the town, and took him to the brow of the hill on which it was built, meaning to hurl him over the edge.

A NATIONAL newspaper runs a competition every year to find the best preacher in Britain. How do they decide? No doubt they use tests like language and theology and simplicity of thought and popularity and interesting illustrations and all that kind of stuff. But if they wanted to measure sermons according to the only example that really matters, they ought to be looking for preachers who make congregations angry! Jesus had only to speak for a few minutes and the congregation were roused to fury. When last did you want to throw a preacher over the side of a cliff?

What did he do? First, and perhaps predictably, his sermon was *political*. I say predictably in two senses. Anyone with any familiarity with the kinds of things Jesus spoke about all his life, like riches and poverty, like war and peace, like race issues and women's issues and the role of law, would have expected him to be political right from the start. And so he was. The sermon was based on a prophetic text: 'He has sent me to bring good news to the poor, to proclaim release from prisoners and recovery of sight for the blind; to let the broken victims go free, to proclaim the year of the Lord's favour.' Those who bleat about keeping politics out of religion have a hard time with the words of Jesus.

The other reason I said it was predictable that it was a political sermon which drove the congregation into a fury was that it nearly always is that which makes worshippers really angry. I suppose that only half a dozen times in my life have I had someone walk out during a sermon; but it has always been on some political point. So it is much easier and more attractive to play safe and not to offend. The result is – well, one of the most depressing books I have ever read is Donald Smith's *Passive Obedience and Prophetic Protest: Social Criticism in the Scottish Church 1830–1945.*[1] What makes it depressing is the overwhelming evidence that despite some honourable exceptions the Scottish Church has failed the people of Scotland – and that it has done so by putting the concerns of power, wealth and privilege before human rights and the dignity and worth of individuals. In the words of the book:

> The Scottish Church was unable to understand that any effort to rescue men and women and children from starvation wages and unendurable toil, filth, disease and early death would have been a higher spiritual activity closer to the kingdom of heaven than much of the so-called church work with which it busied itself.

I wish I thought that tragedy was just a failure to understand. But I suspect it was also an overpowering desire not to upset. Because of course you upset people if you invite them to face the cold human cost of unemployment or world hunger or health provision and demand that they always, as Christians always, face these questions with an overriding commitment to the poorest and the weakest and the most inadequate. The Bible says explicitly that we are judged, judged by God, on how we treat the poor and the weak and the inadequate, and that in any political analysis and in any political party that witness must be for Christians their special vocation, what they are there for. To be the voice of the voiceless.

But it wasn't just political preaching. After all, however uncomfortable that was, they had been having plenty of it from John the Baptist, and the crowds flocked to hear him. There must have been more. There was, and it was *theology*. Do you remember the biggest fuss a Moderator has caused in the last twenty years? It was six or seven years ago and it was about the Virgin Birth. It was about theology. Such a storm that it allowed the Secretary of State for Scotland at the time to quip: 'I would advise you ministers to stick to politics from now on'! Maybe there is something very deep about what we believe about God, something which upsets us very much if we are disturbed.

So it seems to have been at Nazareth. For even more than politics, it was the theology of Jesus which drove them to fury. Perhaps you found it hard to follow the references to the Old Testament as we heard the lesson read; but they are critical. References to a story about Elijah and a widow, and a story about Elisha and a general. Now the point of these two stories is the same; and it is the point of theology which made them try to throw Jesus over the cliff.

When all Israel was dying for lack of rain, it was to a widow woman in the territory of Baal-worship that the reviving grace of God was shown. When decent folk in Israel suffered, it was to a foreign soldier with leprosy that God's healing grace was shown. Why choose these stories? Why, with all the Bible in front of him, did Jesus preach about the widow and the leper? As the meaning of that dawned on them, the crowd turned to fury.

For the message then, in his first sermon, and the message throughout, Jesus' central message, was the unlimited, unconditional, free grace of God. Not just to the hard-working, not just to the religious, not just to men, not just to the healthy, not just to the covenanted people of God: but God's unlimited, unconditional free grace. There is no place where God's grace stops. There is no person who must remain outside. It was that message that Jesus preached from the start. It was that message he lived from first to last. It was for that theology that they tried to throw him over a cliff. And it was for that theology that he was crucified.

For that theology stands in judgement on all ownership of God. Wherever people think God is ours, the gospel of Jesus says 'No'. Wherever people think they have special rights, special privileges, special claims on the grace of God, Jesus says 'No!' 'People will stream in from east and west and north and south, and will take their places at the feast in the kingdom of God' (Luke 13:29).

I want that to be good news for you. I want you to realise that the grace of God is not going to stop at your garden gate, but wants to come right in and claim you and lay hold of you and love you. Certainly no sin of yours is strong enough to put limits on the grace of God. You have come to church today where you belong – even if you don't feel that you belong – now learn what Jesus means by the unlimited, unconditional free grace of God.

But also I want that to make you think. To think of the evil genius of the human race for dividing off, for setting limits, for excluding. To think of the fierce damage we have done to each other by our determination to have a world of us and them. Fifty years after the Holocaust, Elie Wiesel went back to Auschwitz, of which he was a survivor. And at that place of abomination and desolation fifty years on, he, usually a great master of words, could only manage one sentence. He said: 'Let there be an end to violence and bloodshed'. Where else can we say that to the world if not here, where we hear the preaching of Jesus?

Note

1. Donald C Smith, *Passive Obedience and Prophetic Protest: Social Criticism in the Scottish Church 1830–1945* (New York: Peter Lang, 1981).

What grows in the church garden?

Exodus 3:1–6. The burning bush.

ONCE upon a time, I met a man who was a member of our congregation, at least in name. I said to him that he did not come to church much. 'It's like this', he replied. 'I feel more close to God in a garden or on a country walk than I do listening to sermons.' It happened that I met his daughter next day, so I asked her: 'When was the last time your father went on a country walk?' 'A country walk?', she exclaimed with astonishment. 'My father hasn't been on a country walk for twenty years!'

People say you can be nearer to God in a garden than anywhere else on earth. I do not believe that is true; but it does suggest a structure for reflection on the church today and tomorrow. I want you to think of the church as a garden. What might grow in your garden to be a sign of the church?

What about a tulip? The tulip shrivels up and dies, to all appearances. Then, at Eastertime, it bursts forth in glory. Quite appropriate as a symbol of a church which lives by its faith in resurrection. To some, the tulip is dull, and they pass it by – so much the worse for them! But to some, it has been the most precious thing on earth: people have been prepared, as in Holland in the seventeenth century, to sacrifice all they have for it. You can see how the tulip is a quite suggestive image.

The next plant is a lady's slipper orchid. This is the rarest plant on the surface of the earth; this is an image of the church. People who are comfortable around the church forget how strange, how unfamiliar the church looks to those who have hardly ever seen it. My friend was having his hair cut by a young woman, and he was dressed as a minister. 'Are you a minister?' she asked. 'I've always wanted to go to church. How do you do it?' The statistics about church membership and church attendance give at least some support to the choice of the lady's slipper orchid, the rarest flower there is, as an image for the church.

Spreading all over one wall in the garden is a rambling rose. Very pretty at one time of the year, but liable to prick and jag and annoy and cause pain all year round. For the church's role as the conscience of society, uncomfortably, painfully bringing us up against the sore realities of the world, acting as a reminder of the pain of life, should not be underestimated. Each congregation in each parish needs to be a rambling rose, pricking the conscience of its community. The Church of Scotland needs to be a rambling rose, pricking the conscience of the nation.

Seedlings are a vital part of the garden: they point to a church of children and a church for children. The Biblical evidence – in particular the evidence of the sayings of Jesus – for the importance of children in the economy of God is overwhelming. In our garden, we need to cherish seedlings for themselves, not just because they will some day be big plants. Children are not apprentice adults. A garden without seedlings is hardly a garden at all.

What about bindweed? The characteristic of bindweed is that it ruins things. Would that do for the church – it ruins things? I remember hearing the Revd James Currie saying on radio that a Scottish Kirk Session says only two things: 'That'll no work' and 'We tried that before and it didnae work'! Everyone has a bad story about the church. Like bindweed, the church can have a way of smothering things that might have had a lovely life, a way of choking things before they can ever grow, a way of taking over and spoiling everything else. It is really about sin – and sin is to be found in the church. Jesus told a story about weeds and wheat. That story might at least mean that we are not to expect the church to be free of weeds.

Toothgrass may not look much prettier than bindweed, but it is a much more attractive image. Toothgrass is the most widely spread plant in the world: the opposite extreme from the lady's slipper orchid. All over the world, toothgrass is to be found: a good symbol for the church. To think of the church today is to think of the world church. The church is not only in Scotland. We belong with Kimbanguist Christians in Africa, with Pentecostalists in Brazil, with Orthodox Christians in Vladivostok and with Presbyterians in Korea. Their needs are our needs, their gifts are our gifts, their ministry is our ministry. And our gifts and needs and ministry are theirs.

The sign from the garden about which I want to say most is an old sign. It was in 1691 that George Mossman first used it. He was an Edinburgh printer with responsibility for producing a volume of the *Principal Acts of the General Assembly of the Church of Scotland*. For the cover, he chose a design which he may have borrowed from the French Huguenots. The front of the book carried a picture of a burning bush. It may have been from the Huguenots that the idea came, for it was associated with a church passing through suffering. In the Bible story about a burning bush, God uses Moses to bring liberty to Israel. George Mossman believed that God had done the same for the church in Scotland after the 'killing times' of the seventeenth century.

Today the burning bush is a good image for the Church, but for reasons different from those which appealed to Mossman. The reasons come from the story in the Book of Exodus. It is a story about holiness. Moses is to take his shoes off, for the place where he is standing is holy ground. It is a story to make clear that, in the presence of God, reverence and awe are the right things: as the theologians used to say, 'God is wholly other'. Holiness is that which knocks us back and which draws us on; that which can evoke our greatest works of art or which can strike us dumb.

Be still, for the presence of the Lord, the Holy One, is here.
Come bow before him now, with reverence and fear:
In him no sin is found – we stand on holy ground.
Be still, for the presence of the Lord, the Holy One, is here.[1]

The burning-bush story is also a story about calling: about duty and demand and challenge. When slavery is destroying the people of God in Egypt, God says to Moses: 'I will send you to Pharaoh to bring my people, the Israelites, out of Egypt'. It is so characteristic of the Bible that holiness is bound up with demand. God is not only holy but also has a will which is to be done.

Most of all, this story in the book of Exodus is about God: about meeting with God and about who God is. It is the story with the words *I am that I am*. Johnston McKay suggested recently on radio that what God is really saying to Moses with these words is *'It's me!'* It's me when everything is hard and dark. It's me when the skies are bright and your blood is tingling with achievement. It's me when you need me and when you don't think you need me. So quite right that that burning bush is a sign for the Church: for it is that that the Church is for. To help the world to hear God saying 'It's me: here I am'. Let the Church obscure that simple word and it deserves to be burned up in the flame. But let the Church help the whole world – in your home and this city and in this nation and to the farthest parts – help the whole world to hear God say 'It's me: here I am' – then I promise you the bush that is that obedient, faithful Church will burn – but never be consumed.

Note

1. From *Common Ground*, no. 12.

Faithfulness is not enough

1 Timothy 1:14. The grace of our Lord overflowed for me with the faith and love that are in Christ Jesus.

DURING this year as Moderator, I've been learning about some of Christianity's big words.

Faithfulness is important. We went to Finland. It was the 700th anniversary of the great cathedral there: Turku cathedral has been the centre of Christianity, and in many ways the centre of Finland's national life, since 1300. The weekend was filled with celebrations of different kinds, and it was humbling to discover how important a guest to them was the Moderator of the General Assembly of the Church of Scotland. The high point of the celebrations was Saturday morning. The cathedral was filled: the President of Finland and the King of Sweden and church representatives from everywhere and people from all walks of Finnish life. In six magnificent episodes, the story of the cathedral was told in music and mime and dance and colour and occasional words.

As the story of the past unfolded, the story of faithfulness to the people of Finland and to Jesus Christ over seven centuries, the emotion roused was very powerful. If Scottish visitors felt their hearts thumping, you will not be surprised to hear that stolid Finns and hard-boiled bishops were openly weeping. Weeping with thankfulness and pride in the story of the faithfulness of the past.

In this Millennium year, we might wonder at what we could do in Scotland for the story of faithfulness over many centuries. Columba, Margaret, Knox, Chalmers. The faithfulness of this congregation. Much-loved ministers, happy children, gifted musicians, praying people, missionary-minded people, those who have cared for justice for the poor. Even without any tableau of the past, on this day it is easy here to be moved by the story of faithfulness.

But faithfulness is not enough. *With faithfulness we need faith*. Not only faithfulness but faith. For the heart of faithfulness is looking back, while faith looks forward. It was beautifully illustrated at a later part of the celebrations in Finland. When the main speaker was to be introduced at an enormous outdoor event of music and dance and parable, twenty children gathered on the stage and then went down to the audience to lead him by the hand to the microphone: a sign that while faithfulness may look back, faith is always looking forward. Faith is what we need.

Which is what marked David in his confrontation with Goliath. Before the mighty Philistine, David's word is clear: 'You come to me with sword and spear; but I come to you in the name of the Lord of hosts, whom you have defied'. This is what Jesus said to the disciples in the midst of the storm at sea. 'The wind ceased, and there was a dead calm. He said to them, "Why are you afraid? Have you still no faith?" '

The only way to be faithful to the God of the past is to have faith in the God of the present and the future. Putting yourself into the hands of God for today and tomorrow and for the rest of your life. What we need is faith.

Loveliness is important. Soon after we came back from Finland, we were off to Glasgow. To the Glasgow School of Art and the presentation of a silver cross to the Moderator of the General Assembly to mark the Millennium. It is a very lovely thing. I was able to say then that this was the latest of a long, long story of cooperation between the church and the arts, indeed between the Church of Scotland and the arts. For a very long time, Christianity has known that only our best is good enough for God, and that the best we can do in beauty and creativity and art is the very thing to offer to God.

It is just not true that Scottish Christianity – and Protestant Christianity in particular – has been inimical to the arts and to the creation of loveliness. There is plenty of evidence of the flourishing of the arts in Scotland after the Reformation. In all sorts of ways, the Church in Scotland has tried – and does try – to cherish the arts. Think about music and embroidery and pulpit falls and the art of preaching and drama and dance – the list goes on and on. Indeed, our church buildings are often reminders to us that loveliness is important.

But loveliness is not enough. *With loveliness we need love.* Not only loveliness but love. Loveliness is what is on the outside: but love is on the inside. And it is love that we need. St Paul certainly wrote to the church at Philippi: 'Whatsoever things are lovely, think on these things' (Phil. 4:8). But in the full glory of his gospel, he wrote to the church in Corinth: 'Now I will show you a better way: Put love first' (1 Cor. 12:31, 14:1). What is outside matters; but what is inside is what we need.

Was Jesus lovely? Who can tell? There is not the slightest hint in the Bible about what Jesus looked like; although if the old words of Isaiah about the servant of God were to be applied to Jesus, then we read that 'He had no form or majesty that we should look at him, nothing in his appearance that we should desire him' (Is. 53:2). No-one knows if Jesus was lovely or not. But was he love? To that question, the answers overwhelm us. Was he love? Ask Zacchaeus, without a friend in the world until all life changed for him when he met love as he climbed down from a sycamore tree. Was he love? Ask Mary, whose life was tormented by seven devils until Jesus loved and healed her, and who was to bear the matchless title of the very first witness to his resurrection. Ask St Andrew, called first by the nets in Galilee and going on, so they say, to a martyr's death because he knew that Jesus was truly love. Ask St George, centuries later, facing the greatest dangers, so they say, for the love of Jesus, and again going to a martyr's death. St Andrew and St George – ask those who have borne their names since; those who in this place and in the other congregations which are our inheritance have fought the good fight of faith and have finished the course and have kept the faith. Who knows whether Jesus was lovely? – but you can be in no doubt at all about his love.

When your life is judged, the question of your loveliness will not even be raised. But the question 'how much have you loved?' – that is what counts.

Graciousness is important. One of the privileges I have been given as Moderator has been the opportunity to welcome Jean Vanier to the General Assembly. Jean Vanier founded L'Arche, communities all over the world for people with severe learning difficulties and for their assistants. He is a man of extraordinary wisdom and learning and depth and sweetness. And of great graciousness. The graciousness of his speaking and of his listening and of his ability to be truly with you as if there were no-one else to be with; the graciousness of the message he inscribed in the book I am gathering through the year of messages to the Church of Scotland; the graciousness of his giving time to all sorts of guests that I asked him to meet. Graciousness is so important.

But graciousness is not enough. *With graciousness we need grace.* Not only graciousness but grace. For graciousness is about what we give out, what we give to others; but grace is about what we receive: about what God gives to us. And what we need is grace.

Jean Vanier told the General Assembly about his meeting with Philippe, one of the two men with severe learning difficulties – he called them the most oppressed people in the world – with whom he eventually decided to make his life. He said: 'When I met Philippe, I had been trained to do two things very well: I could drive a battleship, and I could teach Aristotle's philosophy in a university. What good was either of these things to Philippe? He needed me and I could not give him what he needed.' As he spoke of this to the Assembly; as he spoke of how God was with him and with Philippe and with us in our vulnerability and weakness, not in spite of our vulnerability and weakness – all of a sudden it was not his politeness or friendliness or sweetness, it was not his graciousness. It was the presence of God. It was not that this man was able to give us kindness: it was that he was able to receive what God wanted to give, and make it easier for us to receive what God wanted to give. Not graciousness but grace. Not giving but receiving.

Grace is what we need and grace is what God wants to give. The unprovoked, surprising, undeserved love of God. That is what grace is. The unprovoked, surprising, undeserved love of God. St Paul was speaking about grace when he wrote: 'while we were yet sinners Christ died for us' (Rom. 5:8). Jesus was speaking about grace when he said: 'The son of man came to seek and to save that which was lost' (Luke 19:10).

Our very own nativity play

Matthew 2:1–12. The Wise Men.

WELCOME, children and everyone! It's time to go over our nativity play. This morning we are doing scene five. That's the one where the wise men come riding in on their camels to find baby Jesus at Bethlehem. They bring him presents: gold, frankincense and myrrh. Now, who would like to be … let me see, who would like to be King Herod? Wicked King Herod?

King Herod has only one line in the play. He says: 'Go and make a careful search for the child; and when you have found him, bring me word, so that I may go myself and pay him homage' (Matt. 2:8). Now, who would like to play that part?

More than you might think. More than you might think want to play Herod; or end up playing Herod whether they mean to or not. He's a liar, of course: Order of Hypocrisy, first class. He has no more intention of worshipping the baby in Bethlehem than he has of flying. But it will sound good if he pretends. If he makes a show of religion. If he uses religion for his own ends.

More than you might think want to play Herod. Want to use religion for their own ends. Church people who try to find in the Church the fulfilment of their hopes for advancement or leadership or being bossy which were never fulfilled in the world. Politicians who seek to have the churches toe the line on Iraq or poverty or the National Lottery. Pressure groups who find some Biblical connection to persuade religious people to support them. All of these people, like Herod, attempting to use religion for their own ends.

Herod's own position is pretty extreme; for Herod's aim is to destroy true religion. To put to death the hope of his people. There has been quite a fuss recently about the resignation of the head of Religion at the BBC: there are apparently intelligent people who believe that the BBC is determined to destroy Christianity. The merciless treatment of ministers and priests who make mistakes suggests that there are powerful elements in our society who wish Christianity ill. The pathetic attempts in the wretched Millennium Dome to mark the birth of Jesus with as few useful and sympathetic references to Jesus as possible suggest that there are those who would be happy to see religion dead. There is no shortage, inside and outside the Church, of those to play the part of Herod in our play.

Now, who would like to play the chief priests and scribes? They also have only one thing to say. 'At Bethlehem in Judaea; for this is what the prophet wrote: Bethlehem in the land of Judah, you are by no means least among the rulers of Judah; for out of you shall come a ruler to be the shepherd of my people Israel' (Matt. 2:6). And then they sat quite still. They had just spilled the beans about the coming of God's Messiah, the goal of religion and the hope of all the nations. They had just spelled out the destiny of their people. And what they did next was to sit on their bottoms. Who would like to play the part of the chief priests and the scribes?

Can you recognise them? Those who know everything and do nothing? Those who know everything and believe nothing? Knowledge and education and study are entirely good things and are entirely good things in Christian faith. But they are not enough. For generations, Scottish students of theology were trained to read the New Testament in a particular Greek text which had as its foreword a saying of the giant of Bible scholars, J A Bengel: 'Apply yourself wholly to the text; and then apply the whole to yourself'. And then apply the whole to yourself. That is what the religious advisers to Herod never did.

Nothing in me is protesting against scholarship. Quite the

opposite; the chief failure of modern Christianity may be seen to be the lamentable ignorance of us modern Christians about the foundations of our faith. But sound scholarship is never enough. It is doing and believing as well as knowing.

Attending church meetings is no substitute for praying. Well-informed opinions on the modern church are no substitute for forgiving people who have hurt you. Fifty years of singing hymns is no substitute for denying yourself and taking up your cross and following. Still there is no shortage of those who will play the part of the chief priests and the scribes.

Now for the stars. Not the star; that's for the stage manager to worry about. But now for the stars – the wise men. Who would like to play these parts? Wonderful costumes, some of the best songs in the whole nativity play, and everyone bowing down before you. Again, there is only one line; but there is quite a bit of business to go with it. The line is: 'Where is the newborn King of the Jews? We observed the rising of his star, and we have come to pay him homage' (Matt. 2:2). Who wants to be the wise men?

On a journey, following a star, searching. There are a lot of people to play the part of the wise men. On a journey, following a star, searching. Last Christmas, there was on television a cartoon version of a story about rabbits called *Watership Down*. Except that it isn't only a story about rabbits: it is a story about people. The rabbits are led on a journey: a journey away from everything that is familiar and safe and predictable. In fact, though they do not know it, they are being led on a journey from all that is deadly. They are led by one rabbit who has a longing, a restlessness, a dream that he cannot explain. But it is his restlessness, his dream, his journey, that saves them. *Watership Down* sold millions of copies not because it is about rabbits, but because it is about so many of us. On a journey, following a star, searching.

Christmas is a good time to break out of the familiar bound-
aries, the tramlines of your life. A good time to dream: to
dream for this congregation; to dream for yourself; to dream
for the kingdom of God. A good time to start on a journey, to
follow a star. Those who would like to play the part of the
wise men recognise that there is so much they don't understand, so much that is ahead of them or beyond them. But that
is the attraction! In 'Ulysses', a poem by Lord Tennyson, an old
sailor longs for more than the sea; he seeks more than boats:

> *Come, my friends*
> *'Tis not too late to seek a newer world.*
> *Push off, and sitting well in order smite*
> *The sounding furrows: for my purpose holds*
> *To sail beyond the sunset, and the paths*
> *Of all the western stars, until I die.*

That is all the parts handed out. You don't have a part yet?
Lucky you! For this story is one story in which none of the
players see the whole play; in which those of us who are left
to watch the play have the best part. For what we see is that
the story isn't about Herod, it isn't about the chief priests and
the scribes, it isn't about the wise men. Like all the stories in
the gospel, this is a story about Christ.

Whether they like it or not, the cruel king and the religious
dry-as-dusts and the wandering star-followers are made to
point to Christ. In this play, they help us to see the one born
at Bethlehem for who he is: the fulfilment of the promise, the
light of all the world, Jesus the Messiah. And those of us who
don't have parts in the play can see this best of all.

Except that, as we watch the play, as we see Christ declared
to the Gentile magicians and worshipped by them, we are
becoming actors ourselves. The story is not just about what
happened 2000 years ago. The play is about Christ, the light of
the world, dawning on darkness. The part that you are being
cast for is yourself. What this play is about is the shining of the

light of Christ on your own darkened eyes.

Watch this nativity play; but do not remain only in the audience for ever.

Addresses

ON ARRIVING IN MALAWI

Keynote Address at a
Vice-Presidential Dinner

I HAVE come to Africa; but Africa has been coming to me all my life.

Like so many others, I have been to Africa many times before – in my heart. As a boy, I used to thrill to the adventure of Africa in books and films: these gave me a taste for African skies and African landscapes which would never be satisfied until I saw them for myself. But more recently it has been books not by British but by African writers which have opened my eyes to what this continent is really like – and I have wanted even more to come to Africa.

The music of the last 100 years in my country has more and more been the music of Africa. At first, the unforgettable tones and rhythms of African music came to our ears through the channel of black American music; but in the last twenty years or so we have had more opportunities to hear the authentic sound of African music for itself. Our popular music and our serious, classical music all carry African sounds; most of all, the music of our churches has been transformed in my lifetime as we have learned to praise God with feeble echoes of the singing of African Christianity. I have come to Africa to hear the real thing for myself, and I hope that the churches of Malawi can promise me a few choirs while I am here!

When I was growing up, I believed that Scotland produced the best footballers in the world! That was never true; and I fear it is even less true now. But I expect that the next few years will show that more and more of the top players of this great international game come from this continent. Already you can see that some of the top stars in England and on the continent of Europe are Africans; and I look to see African teams emerging to challenge even the best South American countries. It is a matter of great sadness to many in Scotland that the next football World Cup is not to come to South Africa after all; and with many others all over the world, I hope that it will come in 2010.

To Africa – and especially to poor Africa – have I come. You know far better than I do, but I know enough to know, that the pain and harshness of poverty in Africa is terrible. I have come here from Mozambique, where I have been seeing the results of the floods in February. One of the leaders in the church there said to me: 'It was because the people are so poor that the floods were such a disaster. With more resources they could have coped so much better.' Not only floods: poverty makes it much harder to cope with every trouble.

I have come to poor Africa from the rich north. We belong together, Europe and Africa. We belong together in our wretched history of relationships in which Africa has been enslaved and exploited and is still exploited for the comfort of the rich world; and we belong together in the lovely strength of our relationships in which we have shared together in a common search for a better world. We meet tonight in the context of the economic summit at Okinawa. In Mozambique, I have not heard any news; but the cancellation of unrepayable debt is a vital part of the future for both rich and poor. I am proud that the churches have been leaders in Europe for this campaign, and I promise that the Church of Scotland will never withdraw from its commitment to transforming the international economic order in the interests of justice and the interests of the poor.

What else could a Scottish Christian say? A Scottish Christian who has read the Bible and knows that God will judge me and all of us not on how often we have been to church nor on how clever we are or how successful, but on the question of how much we have loved the poor. A Scottish Christian who knows that our national poet, Robert Burns, was the poet of the poor. When our new parliament opened last year, there was a song of Robert Burns, 'A man's a man for a' that'. It is a song about poverty: a song which says that you must not measure the worth of human beings by the size of their purses. The real gold is the human heart itself: 'the man's the gowd for a' that'. That poem finishes:

> *Then let us pray that come it may,*
>   *and come it will for a' that,*
> *That man to man the world o'er,*
>   *shall brothers be for a' that.*

I wish I could say that poverty in Scotland was dead as long as Robert Burns himself; but today it still defaces our country too. We are shamefully divided among our own people, and the sad story is that in Scotland as time goes on the rich get richer and the poor get poorer. Again I promise you that the Church of Scotland will seek to destroy the enemy of poverty at home every bit as much as abroad.

But I come to poor Africa with some pride. I want to tell you about the biggest booksale in the world. Each year, my own congregation sells old books for the cause of Christian Aid, the British Churches in action with the world's poor. It may not sound much, but earlier this year we sold books in our own church, in the course of one week, to the amount of £80,000! To do this year by year requires a great deal of energy and imagination from many members of our congregation over large parts of the year: the project takes up a good deal of our time and interest. So I come to poor Africa hoping that we are already friends.

To Africa and to poor Africa I come. But especially to

Malawi. I hope that the people of Malawi feel particularly close to the people of Scotland, for I can assure you that the people of Scotland feel especially close to the people of Malawi. Like many people in this room, I can say that I was born near Blantyre! The visit earlier this year of President Muluzi to Glasgow brought great pleasure. He came to receive an honorary degree from Strathclyde University. I look forward to seeing and hearing more of that university's Malawi Project while I am here.

It's not only the people of Scotland who love Malawi, however. At London airport, I had the fun of sitting in the VIP lounge; and the Italian steward there, who has served the international community for thirty years, was quite excited when I told him we were going to Malawi. 'Oh! They are my favourite people in the whole world! Always so warm and smiling. In fact, I like them better than Italians!'

Let me read to you the opening words of the Malawi section in the *Lonely Planet* travel guide for Southern Africa: 'The tourist brochures bill Malawi as *the warm heart of Africa* and for once the hype is true. Malawi's scenery is beautiful and Malawians really do seem to be among the friendliest people you could meet anywhere.' Over the years in Scotland, I have known many Malawians; and I was in no doubt that if I had the opportunity to bring my son to see something of Africa then he could not do better than coming to Malawi: for here he will find the warm heart of Africa. It will of course be impossible for us to see everything in the ten days we are here, so that might be an excuse for us to come back again some time!

To Malawi I have come, and especially to Christian Malawi. This visit has been arranged by the Church of Central Africa Presbyterian to mark an anniversary as important to us in the Church of Scotland as it is to the Christian communities here: it was 125 years ago that the first Scottish missionaries arrived in Malawi. I am very proud to be able to take part in these celebrations and to thank God for the adventures of these early days and the wonderful continuing history of Christianity in Malawi. Of course, it gives me special delight that Presbyterianism is so strong in Malawi, for the Church of Scotland is a Presbyterian Church. Indeed, I sometimes think that Malawi is more Church of Scotland than Scotland is! It was no surprise to learn the other day that the Malawian High Commissioner in London has joined the congregation of Crown Court Church of Scotland there. No surprise, for a CCAP member would naturally feel as at home in the Church of Scotland as I have already been made to feel in the CCAP.

The congregation in Scotland of which I am minister is full of Malawi connections. I want to pay tribute to my friend Tom Colvin, who died earlier this year, who did as much as anyone to bring Malawi alive to the Church of Scotland. I do not lack information about Malawi – or enthusiasm for Malawi – among my friends! Most of all among my Malawian friends, for I have known many fine ambassadors for your country who have been students in Scotland, starting with the years I spent as a student myself in Glasgow living in the same house as my dear friend Saindi Chipangwi.

For some time I had some responsibility for social and political issues for the Church of Scotland, so I have a keen interest in matters of Church–state relationships. This is an interesting issue in Scotland at the moment as we rejoice in our new parliament, which is one year old this month. The Church of Scotland is learning week by week what is the right relationship to work out between the government and the Church. And so it is in Malawi. We have been full of admiration in Scotland for the faith and courage and sensitivity which the churches have so often displayed in this country over the years in the context of national politics. I look forward very much to hearing and understanding more about this in the next ten days.

It is extremely kind of President Muluzi to offer me hospitality while I am the guest of the CCAP; and I look forward very much indeed to meeting the President tomorrow night. In some countries, it would not be right for the Moderator to be the guest of the state president, but I am happy to be guided by the Church here to accept his kind invitation. The Church must always be free to stand back from government, to speak prophetic words, to challenge and to confront and to measure the government against the standards of justice and peace which the Bible teaches. I do not need to tell the brave Christians of Malawi anything about that. But it is also right for the Church to work with the government, to share together in matters of common concern, and to seek together the good of the whole people of the nation. Call it constructive criticism, call it creative tension, the Church's task is both to challenge the government and to support it. That is certainly what I believe about the Church in Scotland; I think it is what the Bible teaches. I think it must be so for the Church in Malawi as well, although it is not for me to prescribe for the CCAP. In that spirit, I hope that my visit here will help the Church to have clearer and better understandings of how and when it is right to work together with the state, and how and when it is right to speak the prophetic words of challenge.

I have come to Africa. To poor Africa. To Malawi. To Christian Malawi. I have come to pray and to preach, to listen and to love. I thank God for one of the most wonderful privileges and opportunities of my life.

WHY SHOULD THE MODERATOR
GO TO AFRICA?

THE best reason for the Moderator to go to Africa was that Africa invited me. Two invitations had arrived at the Church offices. One was from Malawi. There is probably no place in the world with which the Church of Scotland has closer connections than Malawi, and this was a very special invitation. For it was in 1875 that the first Scottish missionaries arrived in Malawi, and huge celebrations were being planned to mark the anniversary. 'Would it be possible to have the Moderator as one of the Guests of Honour at the anniversary celebrations? – the other is to be the President of Malawi'. The other invitation was from Zambia. 'Our Theological College is fifty years old: would the Moderator be able to preach at the Thanksgiving Service?'

Both of these invitations were very exciting. I had never been to Malawi, but I knew a fair bit about the country because so many of my friends had worked there. Zambia I had visited nearly twenty years ago, when I had the opportunity to help out for three months at the very College which was celebrating its Jubilee. So I was very keen to go. Then, just as we were preparing to accept the invitations, the floods surged over Mozambique. The Church of Scotland has recently been developing new links with Mozambique, and Christian Aid was at the forefront of rebuilding normal life after the disaster. So the visit was extended to four weeks, to take in the three countries, Mozambique, Malawi and Zambia.

'There are different ways of measuring poverty, but in any way of reckoning, there's nothing to choose among Mozambique and Zambia and Malawi. These are among the very poorest countries in the world.' This was part of the official briefing I was given by the Foreign and Commonwealth Office; and I heard the same message from Christian Aid when I went to them to hear of the churches' development work in these three countries. Nevertheless, our experience of each country was quite different. We met remarkable people wherever we went; but in each country one woman had a special story to tell: and their stories are stories to treasure.

In Mozambique, they reckon that the floods have set back development by about fifteen years. Nevertheless, there are some luxurious surroundings and lovely houses all along the Costa del Sol in Maputo. A huge aluminium factory is bringing jobs to many. But the houses and the jobs are not for the poor. In a village of desperate poverty, I took part in a moving little ceremony. There is a project among women and children which was begun by an exceptional woman called Izzy Sanderson; much of the funding for the project has come from a church in Inverness. The little nursery school and tiny self-help factory for simple mosquito nets to be made and sold by the mothers of the children is threatened by the expansion of lavish homes farther and farther along the beach. The ceremony was to bless the plot of ground on which the extension to the school is to be built. It was a moving ceremony because no-one knows whether the extension will ever arise. What would anyone give for the chances of poor women against the rich and powerful? But that little school might be a sign: if it is built, then it might be that Mozambique's poor may have hope.

In Malawi, I was very anxious to meet up with Vera Chirwa. I had met her once before, in a flat in Marchmont in Edinburgh, and until the last day in Malawi it seemed that that was to be my only meeting with her. But she suddenly responded to one of the messages I had been leaving for her, and we had about twenty minutes of conversation. I was anxious to meet her for two reasons. She is herself a singularly impressive woman: it had been difficult to get hold of her because for the previous two days she had been speaking at a church in Dar-es-Salaam about the Holy Spirit, and then addressing a Youth Conference in Malawi on the rights of the child. But she is also a symbol. For she and her husband had been political prisoners in the old Malawi; and Orton Chirwa had died in prison after years of torture. I had been at the extraordinarily moving service in St Giles' in Edinburgh at the time of his death. I wanted to express to her the continuing care of the Church of Scotland for human rights and for Malawi; and I wanted to hear her reflections on her country today. She was encouraging about the state of human rights in Malawi today and about the hopes of their young democracy; but inevitably, like almost every conversation I had in that country, we were soon talking about AIDS. The devastating effects of AIDS throughout Southern Africa I had read about, but had no grasp of their real meaning. Which leads me to Zambia and to Liz Mataka.

There are more teachers dying of AIDS in Zambia than there are teachers being trained. In some areas, 30 per cent of the population is affected. Liz Mataka is the Director of Family Health Trust, an AIDS project which is funded in part by Christian Aid. I heard it described as 'the best AIDS project in Africa'. She sent us to an Anti-AIDS club, where we met young teenagers learning how to help their friends to stay alive in the midst of death. She told us of a victim-support scheme. The Trust has 22,000 orphans on its own register: typical is the woman of 78 who looks after her sixteen grandchildren, all of her four sons and their partners having died of AIDS. We learned about the community health scheme: how do you care for victims of AIDS when even the most basic antibiotics or skin creams are simply unavailable? I was glad to hear Liz speak of the courageous leadership of the churches in Zambia in the struggle against this scourge.

Three memorable women. But perhaps the person who

pleased me most was the Christian Aid worker responsible for the huge effort to rebuild houses in Mozambique after the floods. For when she heard that I was minister of St Andrew's and St George's in Edinburgh, she said immediately: 'I know it. I've never been in Edinburgh. But I know all about the Christian Aid booksale there.' Then she took me to see the results of that annual effort in George Street, and of tireless collecting up and down the country in Christian Aid Week, being turned into walls and roofs for those who watched from the treetops as everything they owned – little as it was – was swept away in the torrent.

REFLECTIONS ON VISITING
SCOTLAND'S PRISONS

I HAVE five words for prisons.

The first is *public*. The distance between Scotland's prisons and Scotland's people is immense. We don't know what our prisons are and what our prisons are like. My chief purpose in undertaking to visit all of Scotland's jails is to help to bridge that gap, to encourage a public interest in prisons and to help prisons feel that they are recognised by and supported by the public.

There was a striking illustration of how difficult it is even for well-informed people to have much grasp of what is going on in Scotland's prisons. When a group of MSPs visited Barlinnie, the headlines were all about how shocked they were at the physical conditions of the worst parts of that prison. The interesting thing, however, was that they were surprised: they, apparently, did not know what it was like. I do not blame them for that; but it is a dramatic sign of how far away from public understanding are the prisons of Scotland.

When I announced that I was going to visit all the prisons, Her Majesty's Chief Inspector of Prisons came to see me. I was quite nervous, for I was sure he was coming to warn me off: who did I think I was, snooping around where I had no business? On the contrary, his visit was a tremendously encouraging thing, for he made it clear to me that the more I could awaken the interest of the people of Scotland in the prisons of Scotland, the better. And that reaction has been mirrored in the reactions of the Scottish Prison Service and the Scottish Executive and the governors and prison staff and prisoners I have met. I have met some of the most dangerous people in Scotland; I have met some of the most radical governors in Scotland. I have met the Justice Minister, and from all I have heard the same: the more public interest in and understanding of prisons, the better.

If I say that my first word for prisons is 'public', then in the present spending climate you are expecting a rather more focused comment. I am a Kilmarnock boy, in the sense that Kilmarnock is my home town. But I have had the greatest possible reservations about private prisons. Some years ago, I moved successfully the deliverance of the General Assembly which committed the Church of Scotland to opposition to privatising of prisons; and I went to Kilmarnock prison with a mind as near to closed as it is possible for a Presbyterian minister to have. I am sorry to say that I had real difficulties in Kilmarnock, because it was certainly a better experience than I expected. I think private prisons are a bad thing, but the evidence I hoped to find to support that view was not overwhelmingly obvious. Old-fashioned as I am, I still think the moral argument is powerful: only the state has the right to deprive a person of liberty, and it is still to me doubtful if that state has the right to contract the execution of that punishment to a private individual or company. I think that underneath that, there lie a host of related issues about responsibility and profit and vocational commitment which will not go away if the privatised model flourishes. I have no doubt that the churches will want to participate in that debate in the future as they have in the past.

My second word for prisons is *positive*. I have been very moved by how much I have seen that is good in the prisons of Scotland. Sometimes, if you read what passes for comment on our jails, you think they are unutterably awful. Unutterably sad they all are, but they are not unutterably awful. There are some terrific things to be seen and heard and felt; and a culture of continued negativity will produce negative results.

However, an opportunity to mention some positive things ought not to be missed.

Like the new Remand Centre at Cornton Vale. It must be as good a facility of its type as you could find anywhere. Clive Fairweather, the Chief Inspector of Prisons, told me at the very start that the three areas for which I might have a particular concern were Remand, Young Offenders and Women. The new provision at Cornton Vale addresses in some way some of the needs of all three. Or the Anger Management Class I heard about on my very first prison visit: four young men telling me how for the very first time they were taking the opportunity to look closely at what was going on inside themselves and they were finding it extraordinarily difficult and extraordinarily exciting.

Positive attitudes to prisons. What other attitude could there be to the noticeably gifted and skilled people who act as governors in charge of our prisons? I have met nearly them all; and I have spent a good deal of time with several of them, and I have to say I am remarkably impressed. Scotland is fortunate in its prison governors. They are all very different from each other, and some have higher profiles than others. But insofar as it is possible to judge, I felt that I met no misfits. There are not many occupations or professions of which you could say that.

The thing I feel most positive about myself, and which I want you and the people of Scotland to feel positive about, is the massive change which there has been in relationships between prison staff and prisoners in the last ten or fifteen years. Fear and intimidation, bullying and violence do not characterise the relationships between prisoners and prison staff in Scotland. For that I am profoundly thankful; and I imagine that nearly everyone is. Of course there are incidents; of course there are difficult prisoners and authoritarian officers; but in every prison I visited there was clear evidence that the regime was attempting to be humane and hopeful, treating prisoners with dignity and respect. In this, as in so much else, what is good for prisoners turns out to be good for prison staff as well: just as what is bad for prisoners so often turns out to be bad for prison staff as well.

My third word is *prophetic*. That is jargon for constructive criticism. Which is jargon for saying what is wrong. It is wrong to keep People Awaiting Deportation in prison (indeed, it is wrong to call them PADs – they are people detained under immigration procedures). It is scandalous that such people should be in prison; but that is hardly the fault of the Prison Service, and I have to say that in the two prisons where I met such people I felt they were being treated as well as was possible. It was poignant to find that these prisoners – refugees and asylum-seekers among them – were the only ones in all my visits who asked me to help them.

It is wrong that prisoners should have to deal with their own waste products night and morning – 'slopping out' is a disinfected term which hides the disgusting reality. It is equally wrong that we should demand the presence and supervision of prison staff at this wretched ritual: who would put up with such working conditions anywhere else? I hated what I saw, and I hope it stops soon.

It is wrong that so many people should be in prison, that so many should be in prison for offences which do not constitute a real danger to anyone, and that so many of these should be women. What perplexes me is that everyone agrees about this, not least those who have to pronounce the sentences; and yet nobody seems to be able to provide alternatives. Everyone recognises that incarceration is always costly, frequently damaging, and, particularly in the case of women, so often damaging to others as well as the person imprisoned.

It is wrong that staff morale should be so low. In a famous phrase, the Chief Inspector described morale as at 'rock bottom': famous because I have heard it twice a day for the last two weeks. The best way to have good prisons is to have happy staff; and in general that is what we do not have. We have prison officers who are proud of what they do, and who are very loyal to the establishment within which they work. But there are significant management issues which must be dealt with if the Prison Service is to be equipped to run the prisons of tomorrow.

My fourth word is *pastoral*. Again that is a jargon word, which I am using in a specific sense as relating to the care and responsibility of the Church. I am proud of our prison chaplains. If my visits have been a success, it has been largely due to the efforts of the Revd Stuart Fulton, Adviser in Chaplaincy to the Scottish Prison Service. I am very glad that I have discovered in nearly every prison fine chaplains working long hours engaged in the most serious spiritual work possible. I have been astonished to find how highly ministers and priests are regarded in prisons: far higher than in Scottish society generally. I am very grateful to the Scottish Prison Service for the clear declarations that they appreciate the value of prison chaplaincy; and I hope that my visits may have done something to encourage chaplains and to raise the profile of their work.

One of the reasons that I thought it would be good for the Moderator to visit our jails is that the congregation of which I am minister has had a long series of relationships with Edinburgh Prison. I hope that I will be able to encourage other congregations to look for opportunities for involvement with prisons near them. I enjoyed hearing one governor giving a real ticking-off to a local minister who was accompanying me because he had never been in the prison before! I do not underestimate, of course, especially as we move into Prisoners' Week, the importance of congregations regularly praying for those in prison and their families, for victims and for prison staff.

It is in the area of throughcare that the Church might be able to show itself most helpful. It is the word which we heard most often in the last fortnight, the word which points to the importance of what happens to prisoners when they are released. It is good that negotiations are well advanced for appointing a throughcare chaplain, and I hope that this may prove a model for other appointments. The question of employment upon release is vital, and extremely difficult. I hope I may be able to help the Church to think of ways in which it can make some contribution in that area.

And I hope the Church will use what influence it has to form the public mind in a different way from that of much of the popular press in the matter of the release of sex offenders. The culture which approves of victimisation and persecution of sex offenders demeans us all. Like most parish ministers, I have some little experience of the results of sex offences and I am appalled and horrified by the damage which such crimes can cause. I resent very strongly the implication that it shows a disregard for their victims if one says a word on behalf of sex offenders. I reject utterly the ridiculous suggestion that it condones what they have done if one says a word on behalf of sex offenders. But the key question is not how we can exact further revenge upon those who have already served a prison sentence; nor is the key question how we can terrify sex offenders most. The key question is how we can stop other children and women being hurt, and very few people who know what they are talking about feel that victimising sex offenders is a good way to achieve that. No, the key question is to ask if we believe that sex offenders too are human beings – however flawed – made in the image of God. I hope that the Church of Scotland will have the courage to ask that very difficult question and to answer it.

My final word is *permanent* – but my words about permanence will be brief. Public, positive, prophetic and pastoral words about prisons will only matter if they effect some permanent change. And the permanent change which matters is not permanent change in Scotland's prisons, but permanent change in Scotland. Over and over again, I have seen that the problems of Scotland's prisons are the problems of Scotland; and only when Scotland is more decent and more gentle and more at ease with itself; only when Scotland is more just and more compassionate will Scotland's prisons be more empty and less sad. In particular, I am speaking about poverty. You do not need a degree in social science to observe that we lock up a disproportionate amount of Scotland's poor people. The reasons for that are complex; but what you do about it is not lock up more poor people, but rather change for good the crippling, destructive effects of poverty on so much of our society.

When I announced that I was going to visit all the prisons of Scotland, I was given some little credit for a sentence which was quoted in the press. I said: 'The degree of civilisation in a society can be judged by entering its prisons'.[1] I was glad to be applauded for saying it, but it isn't mine. As most of you will recognise, it is Dostoevsky's; but what is more important, it is true.

Note

1. From *Notes from the House of the Dead* (1860).

PUBLIC-SERVICE BROADCASTING

Speech to the Independent Television Commission in Scotland

I FEEL a bit like the schoolchild who is invited in to play the piano in front of the grown-ups. They do not expect to be moved by the music, but they hope they may be diverted by the innocence of the performance and the courage of the performer. It is unlikely that I can tell the ITC anything about public-service broadcasting which you have not heard before; but I can hope to engage you by the innocence of the performance and the courage of the performer! I'm going to play some tunes with my right hand, sound a dolorous bass with my left, and then try to give you a proper piece of my very own at the end.

My little tunes are things that I want to make sure are heard in public-service broadcasting. First of all, I want public-service broadcasting to be about sport. Sport because it is so popular, because it gives so much entertainment, because it allows to so many whose lives are barren a sense of belonging and achievement, and because I love it! Sport is a natural for television, a serious claimant for the title of public-service broadcasting, and it is more and more unavailable on terrestrial television. Every single one of my friends with satellite or digital television gave me the same answer when I asked them the reason – 'sport'. Now that may tell you something of my circle of friends, but it also reminds you that sport is a vastly important part of people's expectations of television, and an expectation which terrestrial television finds increasingly difficult to meet. I know that sport is not technically considered as public-service broadcasting; but there are real questions about how the public is served in the whole business of televised sport.

The appetite with which sport is gobbled up by non-terrestrial broadcasters has at least three possible implications, given that it is so very popular. One is that people will spend more on their television than they can afford; another is that people will spend more and more time in pubs; another is that people who cannot view sport will feel increasingly isolated from the mainstream of society. I think it is important that public-service broadcasting has a large helping of sport; and I think it is important not just for my own sake – the Moderator's official residence does not have Sky! But it is important also for the sake of millions of our people.

My first melody is that public-service broadcasting must provide programmes that are really popular: programmes that many people want to see. My second tune is that public-service broadcasting must provide programmes that are really unpopular: programmes that not many people want to see. I once submitted to several publishers the manuscript of a book: the foreword said it was a book written for people who do not read books. Not surprisingly, no publisher wanted it. They took the attitude that people who do not read books are not very likely to be people who buy books! So I do not argue for public-service broadcasting for programmes that no-one wants to see. But I do believe that its role is critical for programmes that small numbers of people want to see. Which brings me to religion.

I have the honour to be a member of the Central Religious Advisory Committee of the ITC. So I do not use empty words when I say how much I appreciate the serious commitment which the ITC has made over many years to religious broadcasting. I think, understandably, that religious broadcasting is very important. I think it is important for those with Christian commitment, for those with commitment to other religious traditions, and for those who would describe themselves as uncommitted – either those whom Richard Holloway calls 'the church in exile' or those who are described by sociologists as those of 'vague faith'. Increasingly, I hope that religious broadcasting will be able to address and challenge and nourish and stimulate those who are searching for moral insights or spiritual realities or courage for living but have not found these needs satisfied in organised religion.

What we need today is deep people. William McIlvanney wrote an essay some years ago which he called 'The shallowing of Scotland'. This is about all of us: for all of us find that life is more and more in danger of being lived on the level of the superficial. My grandfather was an entirely uneducated man who read the Bible and Shakespeare every day. I am very highly educated – my friends would say educated beyond my ability! – I read the Bible every day, John Grisham some days, and Shakespeare never. I have no doubt I am a shallow person beside my grandfather. What we need today is deep people. That is what we need for the sake of society and the world, and for the sake of individuals and their families. Religious broadcasting is a very important tool in forming deep people. A friend of mine was talking to the Chief Rabbi last week and heard him say that the part played by religious broadcasting in smoothing the way to a multicultural society had been enormous and unacknowledged. Making religious programmes is public-service broadcasting.

My third melody is this: public-service broadcasting is broadcasting the news. We have become used to a curious tradition which expects our newspapers to have clear editorial views and to reflect the wishes of their owners, but expects radio and television to be impartial. I do not know how this came about; but I think it is in both its aspects valuable and worth contending for. I want the very strong provision which has been made up until now on terrestrial television for news and current affairs to be continued, and I want it to be continued not just because I am interested in it but because I have no doubt it is public service broadcasting.

That is what makes the *News at Ten* debate important for us all, and not just for broadcasters. Some say that the broadcasters' motives are to take the news away from people; others to make the news better. You know better than I do which is the truth, and you know as well as I do which I want to be the truth. One of the Sunday papers yesterday had a powerful call for new ways of broadcasting the news; but implicit in that article was the view that broadcasting news is important. My concern is that the best news should be available for the most people.

Six years ago, Misha Glenny wrote a book about the former Yugoslavia in which he said that the control of the broadcasting media was the single most important factor in prolonging the war between Croatia and Serbia. Since then, I believe it has been the single most important factor in keeping Milosevic in power. So this week is a very good week to recognise the huge importance to democracy there is in people knowing what is going on. If I want the recommendations of the Sutherland Commission on the care of the elderly implemented in full, as I do, then the single most important thing is that people should know what the state of things is and what the response of government is. The provision of news is public-service broadcasting. If I want, as I do, the Jubilee Year 2000 to be marked by historic progress in the cancellation of unrepayable debts of the world's poorest nations, then the single most important thing is that people should know what is going on, how much less has been achieved than has been promised, and what the burden of that debt is on the broken backs of those men and women and children I visited in Africa last month. News broadcasting is public-service broadcasting, and it is simply necessary. Necessary for democracy, and for the pursuit of justice for the very weakest.

My right hand is at an end. I have played you some pretty melodies about programmes that are popular and unpopular and necessary. But grown-up players play with the left hand at the same time. And the bass line, the long, slow, sad bass line which will accompany all these sweet tunes you have been listening to, is money. Almost everyone agrees that public-service broadcasting is a good thing, and no-one knows where the money is going to come from. I'm sorry to say that I don't either.

But I very much want that debate to be given some energy, so I am very grateful for the ITC consultation on the role of public-service broadcasting. It will be clear to all of you that most of the views I hold could most charitably be described as old-fashioned. So I have an old-fashioned attitude to the money for public-service broadcasting. I firmly believe that there should be public money for public-service broadcasting. Sport for the many, religion for the few, news for the common good – these seem to me to be entirely proper subjects for public expenditure.

Of course, I have no idea how such funding could be worked out. Perhaps I mean a revision of the old licence concept (renewed for the BBC last time round on the Churchillian argument that it was the worst form of funding public-service broadcasting – except for all the alternatives) which would bring benefits to a wider group than at present. Perhaps I mean a new sort of Public Finance Initiative, with public and private money working together. Perhaps I mean some kind of tax incentives to advertisers to make it easier to support certain kinds of programmes. Perhaps I mean money raised by direct taxation. Perhaps I mean that the models being looked at for partnership financing in Gaelic broadcasting could be developed in other ways as well as specialist channels.

I don't know; but I want to be among those saying that this kind of public funding is appropriate and should be pursued and explored – and the problems solved with imagination and conviction.

But then I also believe in an adequately funded National Health Service and in public money for public prisons. So you would expect me to talk in old-fashioned language about the finance for public-service broadcasting.

After the good little child has finished his performance, there is a pause before the tumultuous applause breaks out, a pause during which some kind uncle asks 'What do you want to be when you grow up?' So this is my chance to tell you of my hopes and dreams – my hopes and dreams for public-service broadcasting.

Since I believe that television can be wonderful, and can be a wonderful provider of good things, I desperately want television to be as available as possible to as many as possible; and I want that which is available to be as good as possible. So, of course, does everyone. But for me that means in particular the poor, the disabled and the elderly.

I want public-service broadcasting to be free from state intervention and from market intervention.

I want public-service broadcasting to be innovative.

I want public-service broadcasting to represent and stimulate regional and national identities. The heritage and culture of a middle-aged Edinburgh minister is not the same as that of a young Boston bartender!

I want public-service broadcasting to be a whole package: not just individual programmes, but scheduling and production which meets the needs of the public and not just the needs of the companies or those who provide the money.

I want public-service broadcasting to be a sign to the whole of society, and to the whole world, that money is not the only thing that counts.

I want public-service broadcasting to point to a belief that sharing in the building of an inclusive nation and helping young people to dream and challenging some of the most fearful prejudices of our society are superb ambitions and superb achievements.

Of course, these are ridiculous hopes. But it might just be that the knowledge that there yet lives one who cherishes such hopes – no, the knowledge that there yet lives one who speaks for a whole church, a very significant part of the life of Scotland, who cherishes such hopes – that knowledge might help and inspire you to give your best efforts and inventiveness one more time to finding a way forward for public-service broadcasting. If you can do that, then you will have earned the grateful thanks not only of the Church of Scotland, but of all those who fear that they may be left out of the Britain that seems to be running away from them, all those who have little voice and few friends and not much money, all those for whom television is one of the very few ways out of the wretched lives they have to live. And if you are able to earn their thanks, then you have every right to be proud of who you are and of what you do.

ADDRESS TO THE WALDENSIAN
SYNOD IN ITALY

I BRING to you the love and prayers of the General Assembly of the Church of Scotland.

It is a great joy for me to be with you at the Synod for three reasons.

The first is the warmth of the welcome with which my party from Scotland has been received in this, my first-ever visit to Italy.

The second is that this year marks 150 years of the Scottish Waldensian Mission Aid Society. I am here with the blessing of the society to assure you that the Waldensian name is honoured and loved in Scotland, and to promise you that that affection and these prayers will continue. My first encounter with a Waldensian was when I was six years old and a Waldensian pastor, a bursar of the Mission Aid Society, came to our home. My father failed utterly to explain to me what a Waldensian was, and succeeded brilliantly in passing on to me the sense of brotherly love in which he clearly held our visitor. When I was preparing for this visit, I suspect that I failed equally in explaining to my sons who the Waldensians are; but I left them equally in no doubt about my sense of sisterly and brotherly love.

For 150 years the Scottish Waldensian Mission Aid Society has encouraged and promoted the Waldensian cause among us. But of course, for very much longer, Scottish Christianity and Waldensian Christianity have been partners. Professor Paolo Ricca said in Edinburgh earlier this year: 'The contribution of the Scottish Church to the Waldensian Church has been much greater than we imagine'. I am proud of that: it is a connection which is very precious to us. And the contribution of the Waldensian Church to the Scottish Church is also one which we value and which we look forward to developing. I am very glad that we are about to begin a shared ministry in Turin, and I hope that other shared schemes can be worked out both here and in Scotland.

The third reason I am delighted to be here is that you have generously given me this opportunity to address you. So let me tell you how a Scottish Presbyterian sees you, and how I want to see you.

I recognise in you a church of the Word. The very earliest Waldensian writing rejected the criticism from the Pope by saying: 'We are able to support from the New Testament and other divine testimonies our entire faith which is the basis of salvation and the foundation of our way of life'.[1] That has been the Waldensian way, and so it is no surprise that you were able to make common cause with the Reformation when it argued from the same priorities. It is enormously encouraging for me to see how seriously you take the study of the Bible and the instruction of the mind. My own church needs to learn from you in the splendid enterprise of the Claudiana Publishing House; I rejoice that a Scottish minister had a part in its beginning. It is very much to your credit that you recognise the responsibility that a church of the Word has to words and study and writing and feeding the minds of the people.

But all over the world, churches of the Word are under pressure, and I suspect you feel the same pressure in Italy which we feel in Scotland. There is a particular temptation for churches like yours and mine: against secularism and marginalising to retreat into an authoritarian Biblicism which replaces the freedom of the Word of God with the binding of a legalist literalism. I plead with you to resist this temptation and to be faithful to your tradition. To come to the Bible in a spirit of openness and attentiveness and obedience. To let the Bible be the key which releases you into the truth of God, and not the key which locks you in a dark night of narrow hostility to questioning. The churches of the Word ought to lead everyone else in the search for truth in the name of him who is the truth.

I recognise in you a church of the poor. The famous phrase, which is known wherever in the world the Waldensians are known, is the description used at the time of the trial of 1179: *naked, they followed a naked Christ*. There is something there that is of the very essence of the gospel: something which I urge you to treasure as part of your very selves. Something which you and the world church and the purposes of God cannot afford to lose.

To begin with, it was simply a church of the poor, giving up possessions and holding all things in common. These days have passed for the Waldensian Church; and it has been quite possible since then to be a Waldensian and to be prosperous. But I urge you to continue to be nourished by your roots as a church of the poor in two senses. First, you must be in no doubt, and the world must be in no doubt, that you are a church *for* the poor. The cries of the poor, the poor of Italy and the poor of the world, are the cries which God demands that we hear. We will not be judged on the accuracy of our understanding of the doctrine of the atonement; we will be judged on how much we have loved God's poor children. I am much encouraged by your decision to spend the new money you are receiving from state taxes in the cause of social justice. The homeless in the streets of Turin and those labouring under the burden of unrepayable debt in the world's least developed countries need the Waldensian Church. And you must also be nourished by your roots as a church of the poor by continuing to be deeply suspicious of wealth; that is a healthy Biblical scepticism. I don't think it means that ministers must always be badly paid. But I think it does mean that we believe Jesus meant what he said: *it is impossible to worship God and money*.

I recognise in you an ecumenical church. Again, this is much to your credit, for I suspect that Italy must be one of the most difficult countries in the world to develop a truly ecumenical outlook. In these matters, however, we are obedient not merely to the cultural and historical circumstances in which we find ourselves, but we are obedient to what we believe the will of God to be. Whether we like it or not, the Bible does say that 'those who do not love a brother or sister whom they have seen cannot love God whom they have not seen. The commandment we have from him is this: those who love God must love their brothers and sisters also' (1 John 4:20–1).

You are partners with the Church of Scotland in the World Alliance of Reformed Churches, in the Conference of European Churches, in the World Council of Churches. You do not stand alone; we all belong together. So I urge you to let that ecumenical sense shape your Synod this week. That sense of being an international community. That sense of belonging with Pentecostalists in Zambia and Mar Thoma Christians in India and Orthodox Christians in Russia and – very gently let me say it – with Roman Catholic Christians in Italy. Of course, I know nothing of what that means, and it would be impertinent of me to say more. But I recognise in you an ecumenical, international church, and I urge you, as I urge my own church, in Calvin's words to 'become what you are'.

I suppose I was about sixteen when I encountered the glorious and tragic history of the Waldensians in a poem by John Milton, *On the Late Massacre in Piedmont*. It is a poem about 1655: a poem full of anger and bitterness but also full of nobility and grandeur. I thought then, and I think still, that Milton's prayer that God would avenge the martyrs was unworthy. But when I read the story of their successors, and when I meet the living story of the Waldensian Church today,

I have no doubt that God has done a better thing. He has gone on to the end of Milton's poem and he has blessed the seed of these martyrs and has brought great fruit from them. I am confident that that blessing will continue, as I am that the Church of Scotland will continue to pray for God's blessing on the Waldensians, whom we love.

Note
1. G Gonnet, *Enchiridion Fontium Valdensium, I* (Torre Pellice, 1958).

CHRISTMAS BROADCAST FOR
GRAMPIAN TELEVISION

IN all the Christmas cards – and in several of the best-known Christmas songs and in some of the weariest jokes – the musical instruments that angels play is the harp. I've certainly heard harp-players who play like angels, particularly in Scotland on the traditional clarsach; but I wonder if the old picture needs a little updating. It might be that this Christmas the music which is played by the angels sounds a bit different.

For example, I think the Christmas angels might very appropriately play guitars. The appeal of the guitar is remarkable. It is the instrument which has made pop music: for the last fifty years you could hear guitars on almost every top-ten hit; in the Royal Scottish Museum in Edinburgh, a Fender Stratocaster is one of the symbols of the twentieth century. In the hands of an Eric Clapton, the guitar at its best has spoken for more than one generation. But that is only one side of the instrument. As well as Eric Clapton, there is Segovia; as well as Lennon and McCartney, there is J S Bach. Classical music played on the guitar can be so very beautiful.

It is that range of appeal of the guitar which makes it a good instrument for the angels to play at Christmas. It an instrument for young and old; for conservative and radical. Jesus was born for everyone. For young and old; for conservative and radical. This is inclusive language made flesh – social inclusion born in a stable. Whoever you are, whatever you have been, Jesus was born for you.

Another good instrument for angels to play at Christmas might be the saxophone. It has been the great dance-band sound: the sound to set your feet tapping. The music of Glenn Miller never dates! But the saxophone is also the instrument for playing the blues. That very American sound which does things with flatted fifths and quarter-notes which I do not understand; but which has in it all the pain, all the history of oppression and faith which is the story of black America.

So when your feet are dancing, Jesus was born for you. In the happiest places of your lives, in the best and most exciting moments. And when your heart is breaking, Jesus was born for you. When it is more than you can bear, he is with you. He is born to be healing for your hurt, and he is the source of our joy.

How about some angelic drummers this Christmas? What drums are for is to keep everyone together. If you are dancing or singing, the drums keep you on the same beat with everyone else: when you're marching, it is the drum which is keeping you in step. Keeping you together with everyone else: that's a good instrument for Christmas. When you don't belong, when you have no courage for the fight that lies ahead, Jesus was born for you. Born to bring you in, to help you keep the place that is yours with everyone else. Born so that the sound of Christmas drums might stir you for the fight for goodness and peace.

So it doesn't have to be harps. Indeed, maybe it never was harps. My idea is that the angels' Christmas music is played on bagpipes! In St Giles' Cathedral in Edinburgh, there is a carving of a musical angel – and the instrument being played is the bagpipes!

Was there ever a sound so full of longing? Was there ever a sound that expressed so truly the poignant, trembling desires of Christmas? From the first Christmas to this one, the birth of that baby has aroused immortal longings. From the first Christmas to this, he is the object of the deepest dreams and the most heartfelt yearnings.

O little town of Bethlehem
The hopes and fears of all the years
are met in thee tonight.[1]

The sound of bagpipes, the sound of Scotland, the sound of home. Where we are tonight. Wherever your home is, tonight God comes there, where you are, to be with you.

For years, I have seen Christmas in many languages. For all across the parish where I am minister in Edinburgh, the Christmas message is proclaimed in lights, and the lights carry the message in twelve different languages. Christmas is Bombay and Brussels, the Balkans and Burundi and – most painfully of all – Bethlehem today. But it is also Scotland. Tonight, let Christmas be for the particular loveliness and pain that is Scotland.

The rose of all the world is not for me
I want for my part
Only the little white rose of Scotland
That smells sharp and sweet
And breaks the heart.[2]

Tonight, that rose is a Christmas rose; and Christ is born for Scotland with all her heartbreaks and her hopes. I read a thoughtful article in a newspaper which suggested that it is peculiarly difficult to celebrate Christmas in Scotland. Whether that is true or not, there is no place tonight where the infant Jesus is more at home than here in Scotland.

Where we are is where Christ is born.

A wise old man said: 'What good is it if Christ be born a thousand times in Bethlehem if he be not born in me?'[3]

Notes

1. From CH3 172.
2. 'The little white rose', *Collected Poems of Hugh MacDiarmid* (New York: Macmillan, 1967), p. 248.
3. Angel Silesius.